CORPORATE CRAP

LESSONS LEARNED FROM 40 YEARS IN CORPORATE AMERICA

BY HOWARD HARRISON

First published by Dog Ear Publishing
4011 Vincennes Road
Indianapolis, IN 46268
www.dogearpublishing.net

ISBN: 978-145756-614-1

This book is printed on acid-free paper.
Printed in the United States of America.

DEDICATION

TO ALL MY former bosses, colleagues, employees, and others with whom I've worked over the past forty years: this book would not be possible without you.

CONTENTS

PROLOGUE

SINCE 1978, I have worked for and with dozens of organizations. I was an employee at some, a contractor at others. Working in corporate communications—writing executive speeches, employee publications, shareholder reports, and other organizational propaganda—I got to see a lot of companies up close and personal. I've worked with Fortune 500 CEOs, accompanied sales reps on customer calls, and learned waste management in the bowels of factories.

I've dealt with Finance, fought with Legal, and attempted to match wits with Human Resources. My employers and clients have ranged from medical and biotech giants, to restaurants and food-service suppliers, to chemical and auto-parts manufacturers. I've worked in cubicles and had a corner office on the top floor of Chicago's Prudential Building—and not in that order.

If there is one common trait, one mutual element that links all these companies, in all of these industries, and at all of these levels, it is what I call Corporate Crap.

Corporate Crap comes in many forms. There are the obvious things like meetings, performance reviews, downsizing (although they try not to call it that), and bosses from hell. But it's much more than this.

It's the home office not knowing what goes on in the field but issuing edicts anyway, whether or not they make sense.

It's esteem-sapping exercises like competing for wall offices or having to ask if it's okay to leave early next Thursday.

It's dress codes, task forces, development plans, and fund-raising campaigns.

It's bathroom breaks, break rooms, bag lunches, and cafeterias, including who-to-have-lunch-with or eat-at-your-desk decisions every day.

It's brainstorming, engagement surveys, reengineering, and focus groups; flip charts, org charts, hard stops, and hard-ons.

All of this, and more, is Corporate Crap.

Corporate Crap is not restricted to actual corporations but is practiced in private companies, professional associations, and all other entities that employ lots of people. And despite the emergence of "virtual" companies, online businesses, and other ways you can make a living today, tens of millions of Americans still commute each day to impersonal, structured office environments where they're treated like they're still in high school.

I questioned whether it was appropriate to call this book Corporate Crap given the negative connotation of the word "crap." Then I realized this really is quite polite given that most companies treat their employees like shit. Many companies don't even call employees "employees" anymore, insulting their intelligence in a condescending attempt to show more respect … but I get ahead of myself.

I still do some corporate work, but after forty years of Corporate Crap, I've divested myself of most of it. At this stage of my career, I've chosen to work on projects that have more meaning to me—like writing this book—which has restored my soul. It's as if my mind has emerged from the mud, cleansed of Corporate Crap that went back four decades. *Ah, so this is how people are supposed to live.*

If you're looking for a serious examination of workplace issues, *Harvard Business Review* may be a better source. But there is still an important message here. Companies invest enormous resources to improve their "corporate cultures" and attract and retain top talent. Yet many employees feel as trapped, emasculated, cynical, and negative toward their employers as ever. It begs the question: If companies truly believe employees are their most valuable resource, why do they treat them like crap? I think the answer is they don't know any better. Maybe some corporate wonks will read this and decide to change some things. If not, you can always do what I did—quit and start leading a normal life.

CHAPTER
1
Indoctrination

Soy Sauce Packets

I joined the corporate world in 1978 with a degree in journalism from the University of Wisconsin-Madison. There were three ways I could have gone to start my career: advertising, public relations or newspapers. The only area of journalism I did not pursue in college was broadcasting.

Starting pay for a newspaper reporter was notoriously low and you usually had to start at the bottom, like writing obits for two years. But the main reason I didn't pursue a job as a newspaper reporter was because I worked as one for *The Daily Cardinal*, UW-Madison's student newspaper, and I hated it. I'm not sure which assignment I hated most—interviewing a mother who had just lost a child in an accident, trying to make sense of the goings-on at a late-night city council meeting, or getting grilled by Secret Service at a Republican rally during the 1976 presidential race—but it was enough to turn me off to that life.

This left advertising and public relations. During my senior year of college, I had an internship in the PR department of the American Red Cross. I wrote a couple of newsletters and managed publicity for local blood drives. Based on that experience, Walgreen Company—whose corporate headquarters was in Chicago's northwest suburbs near where I lived—interviewed me for a position in its PR department. Responsibilities were to serve as editor of the employee magazine, *Walgreen World*, and manage grand-opening publicity for new Walgreens stores.

I got the job, which paid about $9,000 a year plus benefits. The sexiest part of the job—literally—was arranging for Miss Arkansas, Miss Missouri, or Miss name-the-state beauty pageant winner to cut the ribbon at the grand opening of new Walgreens drugstores. I never got to meet these women. I didn't attend the ribbon-cuttings. I just scheduled the appearances with their agents and connected them with the local store managers, who did get to meet them. You're welcome.

The rest of my job was mostly writing press materials for the grand openings and employee features for *Walgreen World*. It was not a job I bragged about when I'd go out to bars with my friends, still a frequent activity at age twenty-two. Fresh out of college, single and quite immature, I was more concerned with impressing women than I was with my career at that point. If a woman asked what I did for a living, I was more inclined to make something up.

"I make soy sauce packets," I'd say, for example, thinking this was something everyone could understand and relate to.

"Soy sauce packets!" they'd respond enthusiastically, confirming my intuition.

"Yes, soy sauce packets. You know; those little packets of soy sauce you get when you take out Chinese food?"

"Yes, we know what soy sauce packets are. You actually make those?"

Of course, then it would go straight downhill as I'd be forced to explain if I also made mustard packets, ketchup packets and so on. *And what do you mean you "make" them? You mean you work in a factory?*

Ketchup packets actually would have come in handy my first day at Walgreens had the company used them in its cafeteria instead of the tub of ketchup through which I dragged my tie at the condiments table. The tie then splashed ketchup on my shirt and pants, making me look like I'd been attacked by Lorena Bobbitt.

The dress code back then at virtually every corporate headquarters in America required men to wear a suit and tie. It didn't matter if all I'd be doing all day is sitting in a cubicle pecking at a typewriter. (Personal computers didn't hit mainstream corporate America until a few years later in the 1980s.)

For the next fifteen years, at five different employers, a suit and tie was my uniform. And the only way I got out of it then was to go into business for myself. Before Walgreens, the only time I'd worn suits was to weddings and bar mitzvahs. I could have counted on one hand how many times I'd worn a suit since I was thirteen. Now I had to wear one every day … *every fucking day!*

Today, most companies have relaxed their dress codes significantly. One reason is employee comfort, although even "business casual" seems oppressive to me, an ardent T-shirt and jeans guy. Societal norms in general are less formal these days.

Another reason companies have relaxed their dress codes is legal pressure to have uniform dress codes for men and women. In New York City, for example, the Commission on Human Rights said that employers could not enforce different dress codes based on sex or gender. This means an employer can't require men to wear ties without requiring women to wear ties. They can't require women to wear heels without also requiring men to wear heels.

A more pertinent question might be: If employers *allow* women to wear heels, must they also allow men to wear heels? Before you accuse me of wandering too far into the land of crazy, my wife used to manage a women's shoe store and had a number of regular male customers who bought women's shoes for themselves.

It seems to me employers would be in legal hot water if they prohibited a man from wearing heels while allowing women to wear heels. And we're barely scratching the surface of LGBT rights here. Let's just say all of this makes it more difficult to enforce dress codes today without discriminating against someone.

Learning to work with a noose around my neck was just the beginning of my indoctrination into corporate life. But for a first job out of college, Walgreens wasn't so bad. It was a job in my field. It was a good company. I certainly could have done worse. I could have been making soy sauce packets.

CHAPTER
2
Hiring

Who hires these people? And who hires them?

Walgreens hired me because they knew remarkable talent when they saw it. But it wasn't Walgreens the company that made this determination. It was specific individuals. In my case, as in most hiring decisions, it was mostly the hiring manager, the person to whom I'd report. I also met with his boss and, initially, someone in Human Resources.

These people obviously knew what they were doing. But this is not always the case. In fact, most Corporate Crap is rooted in companies' inability to hire the best people to run their various departments and functions. Or is it the people who hire those people? And who hired them? It becomes a chicken-or-egg dilemma. The point is that the subjectivity required to make good hiring decisions is beyond the capability of most people who do the hiring in companies today.

That's right. I said subjectivity, not objectivity. Objectivity has its place in preventing bias and promoting consistency. Otherwise, objectivity is for robots. Hiring should not be a robotic exercise. Hiring the right people requires *judgment* beyond what's on someone's resume. I'm not sure you can teach judgment.

Hiring is an inexact science, although you wouldn't know it by the abundance of literature and consultants out there to help companies get it right. They mostly just give clueless hiring managers another set of checklists to follow. For example, now, in addition to the technical job requirements, there may be a checklist of personality traits to run through.

"Personality is as important, if not more so, than skills and experience," says one consultant who helps companies identify traits to look for in job candidates. "Skills and competencies can be taught; personality and attitude can't."

She tells companies to shy away from people who are too self-promotional, narrow-minded, negative, apathetic, quick to blame others, think they know everything, have a sense of entitlement … I will stop there. I mean, who *would* want to hire such people? Do we really need consultants to tell us this? Do we need checklists to ascertain these qualities?

First and foremost, a hiring manager needs to be able to judge a person's character. That should be the price of admission. Then you can determine if the person can do the job, how they'd fit in and so on. If you can't do this without checklists then you probably shouldn't be hiring people.

As a human exercise fraught with imperfection, hiring is influenced by a myriad of factors, including things like seniority, politics, nepotism, prejudices, even looks—and not always how you'd think. A study conducted by the University of Maryland and University College of London's School of Management showed a bias against hiring attractive men for some positions. The study found that good-looking men were perceived to be more competent than unattractive men, which you'd think would be a good thing. But many hiring managers also perceived them to be a threat to themselves, particularly if the manager also was male. They'd rather hire someone less competent than someone they're afraid could take their job … or their wife!

"Managers are affected by stereotypes and make hiring decisions to serve their own self-interests," say the study's authors. "This is one reason organizations may not hire the most competent candidates. Awareness that hiring is affected by potential work relationships and stereotyping tendencies can help organizations to improve their selection process so hiring managers will be less motivated to pursue self-interests at the expense of the company."

This is easier said than done. The first time I ever got to hire someone to report to me, I was still in my twenties. I didn't think I'd feel comfortable managing someone older than I was, so I gave preference to people who were younger. I also felt I'd be more comfortable supervising a woman than a man. These things were as important to me as the person's qualifications. I'm just being honest here. The research shows that many hiring decisions are made this way whether people want to admit it or not.

Putting aside the human element, literature abounds with tips on how companies can improve their hiring practices. One thing that's popular is what Steve Jobs called the "collaborative hiring process" or what I call "team interviewing."

I get the value of having input from more than one person, but it doesn't always result in a better hiring decision. I worked in a department once where my boss personally selected who among her direct reports would interview candidates for a peer-level position. She picked all women and we ended up hiring a male bimbo. In this case, his looks did not work against him. But he was a disaster and gone within a year.

Some companies provide formal tests and other assessment tools for candidates to complete. Basing decisions on the results of such tests certainly takes the human element and personal bias out of the equation. But is this really how you want to hire *people*? And the attributes companies seek to measure vary wildly, from "reasoning skills" to "success drivers" to leadership potential.

For some jobs, a test to assess necessary skills is appropriate. When I applied for a job as writer/editor for the American Bar Association Press, I had to complete an exercise that included coming up with story ideas, writing sample headlines and leads, and editing a manuscript. My performance on the test got me the job.

Some companies use the interview process itself as a test. Gallup, for example, uses it to assess how people will respond under pressure. Some companies ask candidates to make formal presentations on themselves as if they were pitching a product. Approaches to hiring vary as much as people and companies do. It's a Corporate Crapshoot, folks.

New tools help companies take hiring decisions out of the hands of hiring managers. These include automated platforms that will both recruit and perform psychological assessments on candidates. Some employ "predictive algorithms" that rank candidates by personality and competence and predict each candidate's chance of success. Some can match a candidate's traits to a company's culture!

These tools use artificial intelligence—an apt term—to mechanize the whole process. Proponents say such tools eliminate bias and thus improve diversity. They also say they cut costs by reducing reliance on consultants and search firms.

You want to cut costs? Hire managers who can make good hiring decisions without all this Corporate Crap. But who will hire the managers? And who will hire those people? We are back to Square One.

CHAPTER
3
Bosses

So, why is this person my boss?

Companies' capricious hiring practices have their worst consequences at the top. If you don't get it right at the supervisory level, all else is lost. These managers then go on to make their own hiring decisions, firing decisions, project and budget decisions, and can personally make life hell for employees. There is an adage that people don't leave companies; they leave bosses. I believe this. A good boss can garner loyalty even if the employee isn't wild about the company. A boss you don't respect causes you to circulate your resume even if you love the company.

I can count on one hand the number of bosses I looked up to during my forty years in corporate America. Most of these were early in my career, when all of my bosses were older and more experienced than I. Over time, the person I reported to was mostly determined by seniority, what was convenient on an org chart, or other factors that did not include things like superior talent, judgment, people skills, temperament, and other qualities people respect in their authority figures.

Reporting to someone—anyone—is demeaning enough. Having to ask permission to leave early or being told what to do by another human being is really hard for some of us. I understand the need for corporate hierarchy. But it is important to make sure that the higher-ups in the hierarchy deserve to be there.

If I'm going to report to someone, I want that person to be more qualified than I am, someone I can learn from, someone to emulate and who through his or her actions earns my respect. I've only had a few bosses in my career who fit this description.

The ability to manage people is often overlooked when companies make hiring and promotion decisions. The person's qualifications on paper—past experience and other background—tend to take precedence. Sometimes company politics determine one's place in the pecking order. Sometimes it's who you know. If your boss got his or her job because they had a prior relationship with the CEO or someone else in senior management, they will be resented even if they have the requisite background.

There are many distinct types of bad bosses: the "credit grabber," who takes credit for all successes but blames others for failures; the "invisible boss," who is never there, like Charlie in *Charlie's Angels*; the "cool boss," who tries too hard to be one of the team; the "bombastic boss," who gets away with bullying and political incorrectness because "that's just who he is." Then there is the boss who embodies many of these qualities, what I call the "insecure boss."

The insecure boss tends to create more work than necessary. Eagerness to please superiors trumps support of subordinates. They can't admit mistakes. They're afraid to admit they don't know something or to change their mind. Most important, they lack humility, viewing such a trait as a weakness instead of a strength—the mark of an insecure person.

Humility means "you no longer need to put yourself above others," says one expert on cognitive management in a piece published in *Psychology Today*. "When dealing with people every day, you need to liberate your ego. If you can let go of the need to feel superior over other people, you can liberate your energy. When you give up the need to be right about everything, you open up all kinds of creative possibilities."

Good bosses are personally and professionally secure. They don't have hidden agendas that get in the way of managing most effectively. They are confident and unselfish enough to value and support talented subordinates rather than feel threatened by them. They know the direction they want to go but are open to input. Other people value their opinions and seek them out. They earn the respect of colleagues and management without kissing ass. They are generally self-deprecating and, yes, humble.

Leaders' inability to check their ego at the door, to subjugate their status, to manage without fear and let others perform without fear is at the root of most corporate dysfunction, according to Kelly Leonard, executive director, Insights & Applied Improvisation, Second City Works. An arm of the famous Chicago-based comedy troupe, Second City Works uses and teaches improvisational techniques to help companies improve their business practices. They have worked with more than 600 Fortune 1000 companies, using the same principles they use on the stage to help leaders change their behavior.

"We teach 'modern leadership,' which is not hierarchical," says Leonard, who hired many of the performers at Second City who have gone on to have successful careers in film and television. These include Tina Fey, Stephen Colbert, Steve Carell, Jason Sudeikis, Seth Meyers, Amy Poehler, and many others.

"Leaders need to create environments that support creative behaviors," he says. "The environment we create on the stage is a freedom to fail. We all have each other's backs.

This is so incredibly important yet so rare in companies. Improv can only work if there is agreement to put ego aside and behave in a certain way."

Leonard calls Tina Fey—who wrote a book called *Bossy Pants*—a "genius leader" because of her ability to surrender status.

"She will surrender status even when she doesn't need to in order to get things done. For example, she once asked me to help produce a benefit in New York. She was the most talented person in the room, but for this event she put me in charge. If she had an idea she'd say, 'I have this idea, but if you already have things down, that's great.' So of course I'd say, 'Oh no, what's your idea?' She would subjugate her status since I was in charge but then reclaim it on stage."

Leonard says that if you're going to work with people like Lorne Michaels, Tracy Morgan, and other alphas, you have to subjugate your status to get things done.

"Tina has the confidence to let them have their ego and their status. She knows what she's got and no one considers her a shrinking violet. But she earns people's respect through this kind of behavior, which is what good leaders do."

And it enables everyone to flourish. Lack of this kind of behavior makes people want to work somewhere else. It comes down to being respectful of others regardless of rank. Many people in supervisory positions can't do this. They're too insecure or full of themselves. Even if they have more experience or talent than subordinates (i.e., Tina Fey), good leaders don't flaunt it for authoritative leverage.

Think of the people you respect in your life. What qualities do they possess that cause you to respect them? Those are the qualities most people want in a boss. It's that simple, yet so hard to find.

CHAPTER

4

Onboarding

Or is it inbreeding?

As soon as you're hired, companies start the brainwashing process. "Onboarding" is the term used today to describe the manner in which new employees get acclimated to their jobs. Experts (people who make a living telling companies how to run their business) suggest ninety days as an ideal timeframe for this process. Some suggest periods as long as two years.

The onboarding process is supposed to allow sufficient time for new hires to meet their colleagues, learn internal business practices, find their way around, and memorize the company's mission, vision, and values. Except for the last item, should this really take three months? I've had jobs that barely lasted three months. I had five jobs my first six years after college. I could have used some onboarding. Nowhere was I given anywhere near three months to get acclimated.

"Let's set the stage," says one onboarding manager (yes, there is such a thing). "Excited and eager, you arrive early for your first day on the new job. Your manager is nowhere to be found and your new colleagues are busy. Finally, someone shows you to your desk and it's littered with the remnants of the previous occupant. Your computer is MIA. No one shows you where the break room or bathrooms are and no one bothers to take you to lunch. This may sound overly dramatic but you'd be surprised how often this happens."

No, I wouldn't. It sounds like my first day at several jobs I've had. I thought this was just the way it was when you started a new job, sort of like your first day of school. I don't think it was a factor in my leaving any employer when I did, although structured onboarding does seem to have a positive effect on employee retention. One study found that employees who go through structured onboarding are 58 percent more likely to be with the organization after three years than employees who don't.

For this reason, onboarding has become another formal and often complicated process in companies today, complete with consultants and textbooks on how to get it right. It's not like companies didn't do it before. It was always expected that new hires would need time to get adjusted. It just wasn't as formal a process.

Academic researchers who study onboarding (now there's a field to get into) sometimes call it "organizational socialization." Some refer to the ninety days as the "incubation period," which makes sense given how many companies treat employees like babies. Others call it the "probation period," which also makes sense given how some companies feel like prisons.

Key to successful onboarding is who new employees meet with during their gestation. Research shows that when new hires meet with colleagues who are positive about their jobs, the new hires are more positive about theirs. But when new hires meet with people who are negative, the new hires are less positive about joining the company. (Companies actually pay for such insights.)

"New employees are searching for validation," says one onboarding expert. "They are looking for evidence that supports their decision to join the organization."

Who selects the folks new hires will meet with? Most likely it is the hiring manager, similar to the "team interviewing" approach described earlier, only this time the candidate has already been hired. The boss selects the people he or she feels will not send the wrong message. If there's a person the boss feels is too outspoken, new hires will have to meet this person later on their own.

What else makes for successful onboarding? "Showing gratitude that the new hire is there, checking in frequently to make sure they feel comfortable, and recognizing their contributions are all things managers and colleagues can do that don't cost anything," says one onboarding consultant. I agree, but shouldn't they do this with all employees?

According to one talent-management firm that helps companies develop onboarding strategies, "Onboarding is more than just new hire orientation. Onboarding is a process. Orientation is an event—the first step in the onboarding process. A sound onboarding process spans one to two years."

I thought ninety days was a bit much. L'Oréal, the cosmetics company, has a two-year, six-part onboarding process. It includes a carefully timed sequence of events that includes meetings and discussions with people at different levels of the organization, training and mentoring, and field visits. IBM has a three-step process that runs through a new hire's entire first year.

Microsoft has a very detailed onboarding process complete with a corporate onboarding mission statement: "to enhance the new employee experience through high-quality, scalable onboarding programs and frameworks that support Microsoft's business goals, advance the 'aspire to' culture, encourage community, and build organizational capability to onboard others."

At Microsoft, onboarding is "everyone's job," not just that of managers and HR. "Peer mentors" provide "safe havens" for new employees to come to with questions or concerns. There is an "onboarding roadmap" with six- and twelve-month "touch points" and a new-employee help desk.

Granted, Microsoft is a company with about 100,000 employees in more than 100 countries in a dynamic industry. But when does "onboarding" end and normal job-related experience-building begin? With employees changing jobs at record rates, is all this upfront investment worth it? Or is it just more Corporate Crap?

CHAPTER
5
Exit Interviews

Don't let the door hit you on the way out

This might seem an odd topic so early in the book. We've hardly scratched the surface of most Corporate Crap and I'm already talking about exit interviews?

The reason is that my first true brush with Corporate Crap (besides having to dress each day like I was going to a wedding) was my exit interview from Walgreens. I was there eighteen months— June 1978 to January 1980—which was not atypical for a first job out of college in the corporate communications field. But I'd have stayed longer had they been willing to pay me a living wage, and as a result, I was bitter when I left and let it all hang out in my first-ever exit interview.

Even in 1978, $9,000 a year was a low salary. After a year I got a $1,000 raise. I couldn't live on $10,000 a year. I asked for $15,000. They said no. I began looking for another job. It didn't take long to find someone willing to pay me $15,000. I gave two weeks' notice.

My boss was surprised. He was appalled. He was angry. He tried to talk me out of leaving. But he didn't offer me more money, so why would I stay? I was angry too. I resented him for forcing me to leave a job I liked over so little money, especially for a big corporation like Walgreens.

In my exit interview, I bad-mouthed my boss pretty bad. Human Resources had told me that whatever I said would be kept confidential. I wondered how the information could be useful if they didn't confront the person with the feedback, but I took them at their word and proceeded to vent my ass off.

On my first day at my new job, I got a phone call from my ex-boss at Walgreens. He confronted me about the things I said in my exit interview, calling it a "hatchet job." I had actually left on good terms with him. Now that bridge was burned, all because of my exit interview. I felt like suing their asses.

I left three more jobs over the next four years, giving me a crash course in exit interviews. I was never as forthright again. But it was hard. When you leave a job, it is often because of something negative, and when I was young, I always wanted to vent about it. I saw exit interviews as my opportunity to vent, to earnestly explain my views on things.

Venting usually gets you in trouble in the corporate world. Venting to HR is almost always a death sentence. HR consultants caution people to be careful what they say in exit interviews. So, why have exit interviews?

Companies claim to want constructive criticism for continuous improvement of their operations. But what's in it for the exiting employee if what he or she says could soil what had been an amicable parting? Not to mention the challenge of not sounding bitter when you feel you have legitimate gripes.

"During an exit interview, it's vital that you be pleasant and professional even if you find that hard to do," says a business writer in Forbes on the "do's and don'ts" of exit interviews. "Remember—this could be the last impression you'll leave your employer with."

The "do's and don'ts" in the Forbes article are based on input from multiple career consultants and HR professionals. They boil it down to five tips for exit interviews.

- **Vent in advance**. This makes sense to me. Get it out of your system so you won't be itching to let it all out to HR. I suggest venting in your car on the way there.

- **Prepare for an exit interview as you would for a job interview.** I don't agree with this one. A job interview is more important than an exit interview. One represents your possible future, the other spilled milk. Your motivation is not the same. The stakes are much higher in a job interview. I guess there is something to be said for being prepared in both cases, but I would certainly prepare harder for a job interview than an exit interview.

- **Be positive.** I agree that you shouldn't be a grouch, but I don't think you have to act like you're happy. Much depends on why you're leaving. It's easier to be positive if you have been offered a great opportunity elsewhere, the company hates to lose you, and they're throwing you a big party in appreciation for everything you've done. It's more difficult if you're leaving because you thought your boss was a jerk, you didn't perform, or you felt you were treated unfairly.

- **Have facts to support whatever points you want to make.** For instance, if I was leaving because I was only making $10,000 a year and I thought I was worth $15,000, I should be prepared to show that other people in my position at other companies are making $15,000. I don't know what good this does after the fact, but having data to back up whatever you want to say isn't a bad idea.

- **Practice your exit interview with coworkers.** This one is over the top. I believe venting in advance and getting your thoughts in order are sufficient. Playacting to prepare for this as if you were trying out for Broadway is a bit much. We're talking about an exit interview here. Have some self-respect.

My feeling is that if HR, the CEO, or anyone else wants more insight into why someone is leaving, they can schedule time with that person without the institution of formal exit interviews. The most telling thing I gleaned from all the research on this subject is that HR doesn't really care what you have to say. Exit interviews are simply part of their job description. If you bring up problems, you just create more work for them. *But don't they want to know what an asshole my boss is? Don't they want to know how screwed up the department is?*

No, they don't. It's just Corporate Crap.

CHAPTER
6
Compensation

Do CEOs really work 350 times harder?

I did not go into corporate communications for the money. I did believe it offered a better chance to make a decent living more quickly than being a newspaper reporter, but starting out I just wanted to get paid for writing while building some professional experience. After eighteen months at Walgreens, however, I felt woefully underpaid. The company was growing fast. I was managing grand-opening publicity for a rapidly growing number of new drugstores. I had significantly upgrading the quality and popularity of the company's all-employee magazine, *Walgreen World*. I felt I deserved to be making more than $10,000 a year.

I felt funny leaving over money because my generation—including me while developing my liberal chops at UW-Madison in the 1970s—eschewed material wealth. This was one reason I became a writer rather than pursuing a degree in business or finance or going to law school. It wasn't until I started working full time and had to pay rent and all other expenses without parental assistance that I realized that while idealism is well and good, you've still got to eat. I mean, I like to write. But writing a piece on a day in the life of a Walgreens pharmacist doesn't provide the kind of nourishment for the soul to replace food on the table.

We tend not to talk about money much at the workplace, other than with our boss when we get our annual raise, which averaged about 3 percent in 2017 in corporate America. We're uneasy talking about how much we make or asking others how much they make. You'll share with coworkers the details of your marriage, love life, or other innermost secrets but not your salary. In my forty years in the corporate world, I never knew exactly how much my coworkers made, and I never asked.

Compensation varies considerably by what type of job you have and many other factors. I'm not going to go into all that here. The thing I think is most worth noting about compensation in corporate America is that the income disparity between those at the top and the average worker mirrors the income disparity in America at large. That is, those at the very top make more money than they could possibly know what to do with, while most everyone else struggles to survive.

When I was making ten grand a year at Walgreens, the chairman and CEO, Charles "Corky" Walgreen III, was making millions. Of course, his grandfather founded the company. And I never for a second would equate the responsibilities and contributions of an entry-level PR writer with those of a Fortune 500 CEO. But was he, or is any CEO, worth that many times an average employee's salary?

At Baxter International, a company I worked for later in my career, CEO pay was nearly $15 million in 2017. Median employee pay was $42,000. That's a 355-to-1 ratio, which is about average in large corporations today. A study by the AFL-CIO pegged the average pay for an S&P 500 CEO in 2016 as $13.1 million—nearly 350 times what the average American worker makes and more than 200 times the average salary at these S&P 500 companies.

The top four CEOs made more than 1,000 times an average worker's pay. This would include McDonald's CEO

Steve Easterbrook, whose nearly $22 million annual pay package is more than 3,000 times the $7,000 a year paid to McDonald's median employee. Easterbrook is credited with rescuing the fast-food giant from declining sales and turning around the business to one of renewed profitable growth. But still, do CEOs really deserve that much credit as expressed in such exponentially large pay differentials?

I've worked with a lot of CEOs. Some I respected greatly. Others I thought were no more qualified than countless other executives who were making millions less. But even among the CEOs I respected most, I never felt the disparity in their talent matched the disparity in their income compared to others in the organization.

Some people who make ridiculous amounts of money like to argue that they deserve it because they work that much harder and/or are that much smarter than people who don't make as much. This is nonsense. No CEO works 350 times harder than the average employee, nor are they 350 times smarter. The highest paid CEOs don't work any harder than the single mom waitressing at Denny's, nor are they any smarter than the research scientist dependent on grant money trying to cure cancer, nor are their contributions to society necessarily greater.

There is no question that the person at the top, where the buck stops, who is ultimately accountable for a giant company's performance, has a lot of responsibility and deserves to be the company's highest paid employee. But a lot of people would be willing to take that on for $13 million a year, and a lot of them could if given the chance. Some might even be better at it.

Everyone deserves whatever they can get in this great capitalist economy of ours. Just don't try to justify your good fortune. Instead, have the humility to thank your lucky stars. CEOs of large corporations don't make decisions in a vacuum. They receive a lot of information to help them make decisions. I'm not saying anyone could do it. You have to be decisive, know the business, and have good judgment. Not any idiot off the street could be a successful CEO. But their skill set is not as unique as their salaries would indicate.

A CEO's contribution to the profitability of a company is hard to measure. You can look at growth during his or her tenure and conclude that the company would not have grown as much under someone else, but that's a tough argument to make given the number of factors that influence a company's performance.

Many people think Major League Baseball players' salaries are obscene. The average MLB salary was $4.5 million in 2017, although some top players make more than $20 million a year, in line with top-earning CEOs. But MLB players have statistics that quantify their relative value pretty accurately. Only so many people can hit .300 against Major League pitching. The population of people with the skill set to make good business decisions is much larger and more amorphous.

There has been talk of capping CEO salaries, raising the minimum wage, and other measures to reduce the income disparity between wealthy CEOs and the peons who work for them. I don't necessarily advocate these things. I'd like to think that with a strong economy, low unemployment, rising stock prices, record corporate profits, and a drastic reduction in corporate tax rates, companies would take it upon themselves to share more of this prosperity outside the executive suite.

I'd like to think that. But I'm not holding my breath.

CHAPTER
7
Office Layout

Tearing down the walls

At Walgreens, I worked in a cubicle. My next job, editing an eighty-four-page monthly magazine for the Hospital Financial Management Association, I just had a desk out in the open, although I spent most of my time in an enclosed work room. My third job I had a corner office on the top floor of Chicago's Prudential Building.

In 1980, the Prudential Building, at forty stories, was one of the tallest buildings in Chicago. My office faced north, with Lake Michigan on my right. I could see all the way to Milwaukee. Today the Prudential Building is surrounded by much taller buildings. But back then, at twenty-four years old and just two years out of college, I had one of the most prestigious office spaces in the Windy City.

The only reason I did was because the company I worked for—the accounting firm Alexander Grant—was based in the Prudential Building and took over the top floor when it merged with a London firm called Thornton Baker to form Grant Thornton International. I was hired to run communications for the new international firm, landing me on the top floor. At the time there weren't many other people on the top floor. Most of the partners and principals of the firm were crammed into offices on more crowded lower floors.

I was at Alexander Grant/Grant Thornton for two years. My next job, as an editor-at-large for the American Bar Association

Press, I was back in a cube. The point is that whether you work in a wall office, a cube, or somewhere else is based on many factors besides experience, salary, or job title. In fact, it's based mostly on available real estate. There are only so many windows and so much square footage for so many bodies, and only so much budget companies are willing to invest in this stuff. While the effects of office layout on creativity, productivity, and employee satisfaction have been studied extensively, most recommendations are not realistic for most companies, so they make do with their available space.

For years, rows of desks surrounded by a perimeter of wall offices had been the norm in corporate America until the cubicle came along in the 1960s. Cubes were supposed to provide more privacy and individualization for more employees along with more flexibility for employers in configuring their floor space. But as cubes proliferated and became the new normal in corporate offices, it was difficult for the pros of cubes to outweigh the cons. Even the inventor of the office cubicle regrets his handiwork, describing the typical cube setup as "monolithic insanity."

While conventional wisdom says cubes offer more privacy than open office space, this is not always the case. Passersby tend to feel more comfortable congregating outside a row of cubes to talk than they would next to someone's desk. This is because the people in the cubes being forced to listen to their conversation are invisible to them.

Cubes also are more inviting for people to "pop in" and visit a coworker because there is some degree of privacy once you're inside. Cube walls even embolden some people to hold meetings in their cube, which is extremely distracting to people in neighboring cubes whose guest chairs will be confiscated to accommodate as many as half a dozen participants in a six-by-six-foot space.

Companies are actually making cubicles smaller, making it harder to hold such meetings, although that is not the intent. It is simply part of a trend toward reducing office space for economic reasons. Data shows the average cube size has shrunk from eight-by-ten feet when it was born to six-by-six today.

In some companies, the cubicle creates a dehumanizing caste system in which people with wall offices feel superior to people in cubes, and the cube people resent the wall-office people. For these and other reasons, more companies are tearing down office and cubicle walls in favor of open-office layouts.

Proponents of the open environment say it enhances teamwork. When GlaxoSmithKline switched from cubicles to an open-office layout "email traffic dropped by more than 50 percent while decision-making accelerated by 25 percent," reported the *Wall Street Journal.* This was attributed to employees' ability "to meet informally instead of volleying emails from offices and cubes."

Most research, however, has found the opposite effect: that open-office arrangements discourage face-to-face interaction and increase electronic communication. In a recent study, Harvard University's Ethan Bernstein and Stephen Turban examined two Fortune 500 companies that removed office and cubicle walls in favor of open office setups. In one, the average time employees spent interacting face-to face dropped from 5.8 hours a day to 1.7 hours, while emails and instant messages increased more than 50 percent. The other company had similar results, with face-to-face interactions decreasing 67 percent and increased email traffic. The authors concluded that open office environments may be "overstimulating ... reducing rather than increasing productive interaction."

Other studies have yielded similar findings. Employees experience more uncontrolled interactions in open environments, leading to higher stress and reduced concentration. A survey of nearly 40,000 employees found that noise and interruptions by colleagues were the worst detriments to productivity.

As a writer, I have always found any sound, even soft music, to be distracting when I'm working. My kids, on the other hand, always insisted that listening to music through headphones while they did their homework helped them concentrate. I thought maybe it was a generational thing, and I may have been right. Open office layouts seem to be the preferred setup of younger workers.

Some people work better with noise in the room than they do in silence, according to a study published in the *Harvard Business Review*. EEG readings of study participants showed "a certain level of white noise proved the ideal background sound for creative tasks." Results also showed, however, that other types of distractions—pop-ins, loud conversations, etc.—have a negative effect.

The biggest problem I would have in an open office environment is just being out in the open. I don't like people observing me doing my job. I had a glass office once that, while better than a cube, made me feel like I was in a fishbowl.

Older employees like me, as well as women, particularly don't like open office environments. The effect on women may seem surprising given that women are usually viewed as more social than men. But a recent study found that women are less at ease in open environments because they are more self-conscious about people staring and scrutinizing their appearance.

Whether you work in a wall office, a cube or out in the open, experts say lighting, especially natural light, is critical to productivity. "If you're in a space that has no windows, people tend to be less productive than when they're in a space where they have access to natural light," says one interior architect. Unfortunately, it is hard to give everyone a window.

New innovations in desks are said to improve productivity. "Standing desks" are popular. These are raised desks that you stand at rather than sit. They are said to boost productivity and health. Recent studies have cast doubt on this, however. In fact, they've shown that standing too long can cause back and circulation problems. A twelve-year study—published in the *American Journal of Epidemiology*—of more than 7,000 office workers found that people who stood a lot at work were almost twice as likely to develop heart disease as colleagues who sat more often.

Physiotherapy experts advise that if health is your thing, take more walks instead. The "treadmill desk" can aid in this pursuit, enabling you to walk while you work. Other high-tech desks include desks with lights indicating when you are too busy to be disturbed, and "smart desks" that capture data on when you're sitting, standing, or away. They can even measure how you're sitting, if you're slouching, and send all this information to your boss!

Perhaps most telling of all the research on office environments and productivity is that productivity seems greatest when people work at home. This goes against the grain in most corporate circles, where supervisors don't trust employees to work on their own without abusing the privilege. There must be a physical presence to maintain control.

In 2013, Yahoo CEO Marissa Mayer made headlines when she banned employees from working at home. She had heard some employees complain that several projects were being slowed by coworkers not being there. She also didn't like the look of so many empty spaces in the parking lots.

"I have nothing against working at home per se," she said. "I don't know that (not working from home) is necessarily the right stance for industry or the world at large. It was just the right thing for us at that moment." She added that "people are more collaborative and more inventive when they come together."

The research says otherwise, but this is the mantra of most corporations—how to get people to work more effectively together. This is really what is behind most efforts to tear down the walls and move to more open office layouts.

"The corporate world pushes extroversion on people, most often through a relentless meetings culture," says Leonid Bershidsky, a Bloomberg business writer. "Some find that so uncomfortable they unconsciously try to minimize human contact."

As an introvert, I can attest to this—and will have much more to say about it in a later chapter.

CHAPTER

8

Performance Reviews

"I've seen the future; it's a bald-headed man from New York!"

The day I learned how worthless performance reviews are was the day I got fired from Alexander Grant immediately after receiving a stellar performance review.

There is a scene in the movie *Lost in America* with Albert Brooks that will forever remind me of my departure from Alexander Grant. Brooks' character, a young and talented advertising executive, goes to a meeting thinking he is about to be promoted. Instead, his boss tells him the firm just won the Ford account and wants him to move to New York to work under a bald nebbish in a bad suit. Enraged, Brooks quits, screaming on his way out that no one should trust the firm with their future. "I've seen the future; it's a bald-headed man from New York!"

My story is similar. When I joined the accounting firm of Alexander Grant in 1980, lawyers, doctors, and certified public accountants did not advertise. It was thought to be beneath the dignity of such professions. In the early '80s this began to change. So the firm brought in this bald-headed marketing consultant from New York to pitch the partners on an ad campaign. I didn't like the guy. He reminded me of a snake oil salesman. I made no attempt to hide how I felt because a) I was still young and stupid, and b) he was just a consultant.

On my two-year anniversary, my boss gave me a stellar performance review. He praised my work in creating a global communications platform from scratch for Grant Thornton International following Alexander Grant's merger with Thornton Baker. He said he was looking forward to seeing me play a lead role in the firm's new marketing initiative with the consultant from New York.

A week later, my boss told me I was being let go. The partners were so taken with the guy from New York that they made him a principal in the firm and put him over my boss. The guy said he wanted to bring in his own people. Like Albert Brooks, I saw the future, and it was a bald-headed man from New York. That stellar performance review I had just received meant nothing.

Today, thirty-five years later, most HR professionals, managers, and employees acknowledge that annual performance reviews are worthless. According to a study by research firm CEB (formerly known as the Corporate Executive Board):

- 95% of managers are dissatisfied with their organizations' performance review process
- 90% of HR professionals don't believe their companies' performance reviews provide accurate information
- 66% of employees say the performance review process interferes with their productivity
- 65% say it isn't relevant to their jobs
- 59% feel performance reviews are not worth the time invested
- 56% say they do not receive feedback on what to improve

"Our research shows that individual performance ratings have absolutely zero correlation with actual business results," says one CEB researcher involved in the study. "And they're incredibly time-consuming."

Managers in the survey estimated that they spend more than 200 hours a year on performance management activities and that their employees each spend forty hours. Performance reviews also "set up an uncomfortable dynamic between managers and employees in which one person is judge and jury for the other."

An increasing number of companies, to their credit, are abandoning annual performance reviews in favor of systems that provide more timely feedback. Providing more frequent feedback is clearly more effective than suppressing feedback in favor of documenting everything for a yearly sit-down. According to the CEB study, 12 percent of the Fortune 1000 companies have moved in this direction, including Microsoft, General Electric, Netflix, Accenture, and Adobe.

"People are realizing that doing anything annually, whether it's a performance review, engagement survey, or goal-setting, makes no sense," says one HR consultant.

Of course, the most effective feedback is immediate. Think of a hitter in baseball who hits a long drive he's sure is a home run, so he stands at the plate admiring it instead of running to first base. When the ball falls short and the hitter's lack of hustle results in a 400-foot single, should the manager wait until the end of the season to mention it? He will probably mention it as soon as the guy gets his lazy ass back to the dugout, and if the manager has any balls, he'll send the guy home.

Why does corporate America have to be so constipated when it comes to assessing and providing feedback on performance? One reason is because most supervisors can't manage "in the moment." If a supervisor can't provide real-time feedback, then they shouldn't be managing people. Annual performance reviews, or any regularly scheduled feedback meetings, let such managers off the hook.

I had a supervisor once who scheduled weekly "check-ins" that she usually canceled at the last minute as they took on lowest-priority status in a busy corporate communications department. When we did meet, there was usually nothing we had to discuss anyway. It became just another "standing" meeting on the calendar that hemmed us in.

I believe most standing meetings—whether annually, quarterly, monthly, or weekly—become a bane for employees. Meetings in general are among the most irritating features of corporate life. They also represent companies' biggest time-suck.

9

Meetings

Companies' biggest time-suck

When asked what the biggest time-waster is in their workday, most employees say meetings. A Harris Poll survey showed the average American worker spends more than nine hours a week preparing for or sitting through meetings, and this seems low to me. For some in corporate America, life is nothing but an endless series of meetings. It has been estimated that approximately 11 million meetings are held each day in the United States, and this, too, seems low. It also has been estimated that a third of these meetings are unproductive. I don't know how they measure productivity, but I'd have thought at least two-thirds of all meetings would be deemed unproductive. Another statistic: unproductive meetings cost U.S. business about $40 billion a year.

There are so many different kinds of meetings that I should clarify what kind we're talking about. There are the big meetings— the conferences, conventions, and trade shows—and all the workshops, symposia, seminars, and panel discussions that come with them. I'm not talking about these meetings. There are one-on-one meetings, where you only meet with one or two people. There are lunch meetings, where you "do lunch" with someone and try to take care of business at the same time. I'm not talking about any of these meetings either.

I'm talking about all the group meetings we attend every day in offices and conference rooms across corporate America—the staff meetings, team meetings, department meetings, and others. Many of these are regularly scheduled, like the meeting every Monday morning where you go around the table and everyone talks about what they're working on. These meetings tend to outgrow their usefulness over time, becoming an obligation that employees come to loathe.

Conference calls, or teleconferences, are big today because the technology allows a virtually unlimited number of people from almost anywhere in the world to come together for very little cost. It may be the middle of the night for some and the butt-crack of dawn for others, but the cost and logistics of getting all these people together in person would be prohibitive for most organizations.

Time coaches—people who help companies and employees use their time more efficiently—suggest prioritizing the agenda for conference calls so people who don't have to be on the whole call can drop off when the subject matter is no longer relevant to them. Failure to do this risks people losing focus and turning to other activities. For example, in one survey, 6 percent of employees admitted falling asleep during conference calls. Even more popular: doing other work, sending emails and texts, eating or making food, going to the bathroom, checking social media, playing video games, shopping online, and exercising.

When it comes to in-person meetings, there is an avalanche of material on how to improve "meeting productivity." I will try to summarize some of this insight.

One thing all the experts agree on is that companies have too many meetings. They also recommend shorter meetings. Some suggest limiting them to fifteen minutes and setting a timer. When the timer goes off, the meeting is over, period. Of course, if you didn't accomplish what you wanted to, you will just have to schedule another meeting, which seems counterproductive.

A big problem at group meetings is too many people. "Attending meetings is not a badge of honor," writes Kristin Gill in her book *Think Like Google*. Google has a ten-person limit at meetings. Restricting attendance to just essential participants optimizes time spent and leads to quicker decisions. Inviting people to be nice or as a development experience doesn't do them any favors either. Few things are more boring than sitting through a meeting you don't need to attend.

The people who call meetings don't know how to lead meetings, experts say. They suggest hiring a professional "facilitator," described as a person "who contributes structure and process to interactions so groups are able to function effectively and make high-quality decisions."

I don't think companies should have to pay a professional to run their meetings, although someone must be able to manage the loudmouth/blowhard/know-it-all who sucks the energy out of most meetings. In lieu of actual knowledge or insight, these people try to be the loudest voice in the room to drown out any other ideas that might expose their shallowness. One organizational psychologist describes their bellicose ramblings as "proxies for expertise."

At meetings where not everyone knows each other, it is important to make introductions, not just to break the ice but so everyone knows who they're dealing with around the table. This makes sense. But don't you just hate those meetings where everyone has to say something about themselves? It eats up a lot of time, which becomes a bigger issue given that more than a third of all meetings start late. This reflects a common behavioral deficiency in our society: the inability to be on time. One person being late to a meeting often holds up the whole thing.

There have been studies on the effects of caffeine at meetings. I always liked to bring a cup of coffee to a meeting if there wasn't already coffee in the room. If the meeting was after lunch, this was almost a necessity. But research says this might not be a good idea. One study showed that men who drank coffee at meetings performed worse than men who didn't. Of course, the same study said women who drank coffee at meetings performed better. As for food at meetings, many people find it offensive. If you need to feed people, the meeting is too long.

Most employees think it is rude to answer phone calls or write or read emails or texts during a meeting. So why do they do it? That would be a good study. Today people also bring laptops, tablets, and other gadgets to meetings. Research suggests banning all these devices. Good luck with that.

Some productivity experts suggest banning chairs from meetings. That's right. Proponents of the "stand-up meeting" say standing makes people uncomfortable, giving them an incentive to get the meeting over with so they can go sit down. Meetings will go faster, and people will be less inclined to have them. Hey, why not crank up the heat while you're at it? That would be some real Corporate Crap!

CHAPTER

10

Mission/Vision/Values

Semantics on Steroids

Among my least favorite meetings to attend during my forty years in corporate America were those devoted to helping companies write or recast their "mission, vision, and values" statements. As a corporate wordsmith, I was invited to participate in a number of these games of high-level corporate semantics. Companies think these carefully crafted declarations of self-righteousness say something unique about them and help define their "cultures." The reality is that it is hard to distinguish these things from one company to the next, and most people don't care about them outside the executive suite.

Inside corporate boardrooms, however, a company's mission, vision, and values statements take on exaggerated importance. Some organizations view them as if they were the Ten Commandments, which is appropriate given that the process to create them is no less arduous than Moses could have endured. Corporate executives, middle managers, and consultants spar over every word as if the future of the company rode on which unnecessary hyperbolic adjective to include.

It usually takes weeks if not months of meetings and iterations, consuming enough flip charts to raze a forest, before the final statements are approved. Every member of senior management has to weigh in, as do their admins, spouses, and sometimes extended families. But it doesn't stop there.

Given all the time invested in creating these statements, there must be an even greater investment in fanfare to promote them. More meetings and brain cells (not to mention flip charts) are consumed to develop detailed action plans on how to communicate to employees, shareholders, customers, and other stakeholders why these words are newsworthy.

Personally, I was forced to build this shit into annual report copy, executive speeches, and everything else I was working on—and forced is not an overstatement. Employee announcements, department meetings, posters, banners, table tents, wallet cards, napkins, notepads, and coffee mugs are some of the other channels through which companies try to drum this stuff into people's heads.

I'm not saying companies shouldn't have mission, vision, and values statements. I think they are nice "for the record" declarations of what a company is about. But that's the extent of their value. Here are the general definitions:

A company's **mission statement** is basically its statement of purpose (although some companies have an actual "statement of purpose" in addition to a mission statement). It describes or alludes to the company's business—what it does—and its general strategic direction.

A **vision statement** describes the future desired state of the company—where it wants to go and what it seeks to accomplish. It is supposed to be aspirational and inspirational, particularly for employees.

A **values statement** tells the world what the company stands for. It provides a moral compass to guide decision-making and establish a behavioral standard for everything an organization does.

The format and detail of these statements vary. Here are the mission, vision, and values statements of Centegra Health System, a network of hospitals, doctors, and clinics serving the northwest suburbs of Chicago:

- **Mission:** We inspire and engage our community in their health and wellness.
- **Vision:** To be the community leader for a better life.
- **Values:** We commit to serving with genuine respect, passionate caring and a joyful spirit.

Now, here are the mission, vision, and values statements of Coca-Cola:

Mission
- To refresh the world …
- To inspire moments of optimism and happiness …
- To create value and make a difference.

Vision
- **People:** Be a great place to work where people are inspired to be the best they can be.
- **Portfolio:** Bring to the world a portfolio of quality beverage brands that anticipate and satisfy people's desires or needs.
- **Partners:** Nurture a winning network of customers and suppliers, together we create mutual, enduring value.
- **Planet:** Be a responsible citizen who makes a difference by helping build and support sustainable communities.
- **Profit:** Maximize long-term return to shareholders while being mindful of our overall responsibilities.

- **Productivity:** Be a highly effective, lean, and fast-moving organization.

Values
- **Leadership:** The courage to shape a better future
- **Collaboration:** Leverage collective genius
- **Integrity:** Be real
- **Accountability:** If it is to be, it's up to me
- **Passion:** Committed in heart and mind
- **Diversity:** As inclusive as our brands
- **Quality:** What we do, we do well

A few comments: In Coca-Cola's mission statement, only the word "refresh" hints that this is a beverage company. Otherwise, it could apply to a lot of companies in all kinds of industries. In Coca-Cola's vision statement, it is remarkable that each element starts with the letter "P." I bet Pepsi wishes they thought of this. I guess they couldn't get this gimmick to work with the values statement.

The Kellogg food company of Battle Creek, Michigan (the town literally smelled like corn flakes when I drove through it some years ago), has both a purpose and a mission statement. Its mission statement: "Kellogg is a global company committed to building long-term growth in volume and profit and to enhancing its worldwide leadership position by providing nutritious food products of superior value." Its purpose: "Nourishing families so they can flourish and thrive."

The mission clearly is speaking more to investors, the purpose to folks like you and me. I like the purpose better, don't you?

No matter how much time and energy a company spends on its mission, vision, and values statements, these statements are unlikely to differentiate the company because its competitors will surely have similar statements. "Nordstrom works relentlessly to give customers the most compelling shopping experience possible," the retailer declares in its mission statement—as do the mission statements of virtually everyone else in the retail industry.

I have done work for a number of companies in health care. They all have basically the same mission statement. Here's Merck's, a little wordier than most but whose message could have been picked out of the hat: "With our research-driven specialty businesses, we help patients, customers, partners, and our communities around the world to live a better life. We deliver entrepreneurial success through innovation."

Clearly Merck wants to highlight its research and development, as do all pharmaceutical and health-care technology companies. Take out the word "patients" from Merck's mission statement and a chemical manufacturer could make the same claim. In fact, take out the word "patients" and it could apply to companies in any number of industries. Everyone—from health-care companies to landscape contractors—wants to help "the world to live a better life."

Ah, but the wasted energy dedicated to this stuff goes even deeper. Some companies fall all over themselves trying to tie each employee's individual and departmental goals to the company's mission. First you tie the CEO's goals to the mission. Then you tie his or her direct reports' goals to the CEO's goals, and so on down to Joe on the assembly line. This way "everyone's performance objectives are aligned with the company's mission." Doesn't that sound nice?

In my experience, I have seen the effort to line everything up this way cause managers to lose their grasp of reality. The process takes on a life of its own, vastly complicating rather than clarifying people's roles.

If you don't already know what your company does and what your role is, I'm not sure some flowery mission or vision statement is going to help you. The same goes for values. I try to live by the Golden Rule. Those are my values. Whatever a company's values are, it can't expect them to become part of the company's DNA because of words on a wallet card. A Gallup poll found that less than 30 percent of employees believe in their employer's stated values, let alone think about how those values apply to them.

"If we want individuals to align themselves with organization values, first we as leaders need to get our perspective right," says Michael Crossland, a frequent speaker on values and their effect on businesses. "Are we being leaders or bosses? A boss says, 'Go do it.' A leader says, 'Let's do it.' Leadership is not about what we can get them to do for us. It's about what we can give back to the team."

This sounds a lot like President Kennedy's famous line, "Ask not what your country can do for you. Ask what you can do for your country." I can only imagine the speechwriters in JFK's Oval Office sparring over those words!

I've never believed in "group writing," which is how mission, vision, and values statements are created. Wherever I've worked, had the company asked me to write its mission, vision, and/or values statements myself, I could have done so in an hour, and it would not have had any more or less effect on the company's performance or stock price. When I think of all the dissension, yelling, and name-calling in corporate offices and boardrooms over the wording of mission/vision/values statements, it makes me laugh—now. It used to make me cry. One thing I learned: companies take semantics very seriously.

CHAPTER
11
The "E" Word

An employee by any other name ...

Companies take semantics so seriously that many don't even call their employees "employees" anymore. Apple calls its employees "geniuses." Disney calls theirs "cast members." At Cabela's they are "outfitters," at Starbucks they are "baristas," and at Subway "sandwich artists." At Trader Joe's they are "mates" except for the store manager, who is "captain."

At least these companies are trying to be more playful or descriptive in defining people's jobs. Companies that call employees "associates" or "team members" because they think it will make employees feel more vested in the organization or better about themselves are the ones full of Corporate Crap.

I wrote for one CEO who would change the word "employee" to "team member" in everything I wrote for him—whether it was his column in the employee newsletter or a speech to stockholders. "Employees" was often the better word choice, especially in the latter instance when addressing an outside audience, but he was relentless and unwavering on this.

"Show me an organization that hires 'employees' to achieve company goals and I'll show you a company that's low on morale and high in turnover," says one Human Resources consultant quite seriously. "It's not that having employees is necessarily a bad thing. But it does stunt your ability to create a more accountable, open, and honest work environment. Plus you're limiting your company's ability to create an environment where people want to go every day, give their best effort, and most importantly, tell others about it."

To be fair, this consultant defines "team members" and "employees" differently and assigns different qualities to each to help companies identify "team players," who are good for the business, versus "employees," who will "stunt your ability to create a more accountable, open, and honest work environment." That's different than companies that insult employees' intelligence by using semantics to make them feel more empowered or that think the word "employee" is demeaning.

"I've never understood what's so bad about being an employee," says Vickie, whose company began calling employees "associates" a few years ago. "Yes, many of us get meaning from our work, but it's still basically a financial relationship. I doubt any of us would be there if we didn't get paid."

"The word 'employee' does not mean 'slave,'" says one HR manager. "Yet I believe this perception is why some organizations call their employees 'associates,' so they won't feel like slaves. What companies should be more focused on is treating employees with dignity and respect. You can call them kings and queens if you want, but if they are not treated fairly or feel undervalued, what good are those titles?"

The HR director of another Fortune 500 company agrees. "It doesn't matter what you call people. Your actions are more meaningful. If you're going to be cute with what you call employees, you better deliver on whatever promise you think you're making. You're better off calling them employees but doing all the upstream stuff you think the other names indicate. You'll end up in the same place, without risking looking like a moron."

Companies do risk cynicism and ridicule when they make a big deal out of what they call their employees. For most it represents a change they feel they need to announce as if it were a major acquisition or change in senior management. Then when nothing else changes, the company gets eye-rolls.

"We roll our eyes because they call us associates, but they sure don't treat us like partners," says Ellie. "Our company made major changes in the software we use to do our jobs and didn't even consult with us. If you're not even going to consult with me on the tools I need to do my job, then you might as well call me an employee because now you're not only disrespectful, you're also a hypocrite."

"The word 'associate' makes me cringe," says Gretchen. "Are we part of some organized crime circle?"

"I worked for an organization that decided to begin calling employees 'teammates,'" says Steve. "There was no explanation why, no other outward changes, just 'teammates' instead of 'employees.' Within six months I had to lay off hundreds of 'teammates' when the company started having financial issues. I don't think being called 'teammates' helped them feel any better."

The name game is more likely to cause employees to lose respect for the company than gain respect for it or themselves. The fact is that most employees don't care what they're called.

"When people come to me with a complaint about their employer, it's usually not about their title," says an employment lawyer. "It's about how they were treated—simple as that."

"Generally the less bullshit the better when it comes to managing people," says Phil. "They're smart enough to see through it."

The same argument can be made for insisting on calling coworkers "colleagues," bosses "supervisors," and customers "guests." It doesn't matter. It's just Corporate Crap.

CHAPTER
12
Faking It

Shaking Hands (and other stupid protocols by which you're judged)

There is no end to how much we have to "fake it" in the office or workplace. We have to pretend to like or respect people we don't. We have to fake interest in how people spent their weekends. We join in group praise for others' successes (however loosely defined) even if we think the work sucked. I could go on forever. Acting lessons should become standard fare at business schools.

Faking is not the same thing as lying. Faking is more a necessary evil in the business world. When you call in sick when you're not, that's lying. Being polite to rude clients or customers because you have to, that's faking it. Sometimes faking it is good for you. They've done studies that show when you fake being happy, you actually end up being happier than people who don't fake it.

A critical skill in the business world is the ability to fake being interested in what someone else is saying when you are actually bored out of your mind. The key is what researchers call "gaze," as in your ability to gaze into the person's eyes while they are talking to pretend you're interested. Since you usually aren't, *gaze* can turn into *glaze* quite easily, as in your eyes glazing over, if you're not careful.

Shaking hands, for me, is faking it because I never want to shake anyone's hand, but I am compelled to because of what may be our stupidest custom. You can be sitting in the cafeteria eating a tuna sandwich and someone will come up to you and stick out their hand. I would say, "Hey, good to see you," nod toward my messy hands, and wink, and most people would get it and back off. But some people expect a return handshake no matter what. Do they really want to shake a hand with tuna fish on it? Probably not, but they don't think about it. It is a robotic reflex response devoid of reason.

Or how about the awkwardness of dealing with people who unabashedly go for the hug and/or cheek rub/side kiss? To rebuff makes you seem like the bad guy. Why do we have to physically touch people to greet them? Why is this shit so important? Instead of making sure there are dispensers of Purell throughout the office, why can't we at least reconsider the tradition of hand shaking? Why can't we just make eye contact, smile, and greet verbally? Why do we have to grab at each other? Why? Because you're rude if you don't, that's why. This is Corporate Crap at its purest.

Back in the day, and probably even still today, companies actually considered the quality of a person's handshake in their hiring decision. "He's got a good, firm handshake," they'd say, noting that as a point in the candidate's favor.

In addition to being expected to automatically stick out your hand whenever someone offers theirs, you also are expected to initiate the handshake if you are the one doing the approaching. On the surface, it may sound like it would be easy not to do this since you're the one initiating the action. But in practice it is difficult. That's how conditioned we are to this ridiculous custom.

Think about it. You have a meeting with someone you don't know well or perhaps have never met. Their assistant announces you, and you walk into the person's office, where they are waiting for you. Just try walking in and not extending your hand. It's hard. Of course, usually they will automatically extend theirs before you can think about it, so you normally don't have to make this conscious decision.

In the tuna fish example, you have a legitimate excuse for not shaking the person's hand. Your hands have food on them. It amazes me how even in this situation people still insist on shaking your hand. But at least you have an excuse for trying to get out of it. In most cases, you don't have a good excuse besides the obvious non-hygienic aspects of it, and failure to shake someone's hand will likely be taken personally. So you do it, like all the other things you do that don't make sense— you do them because it's not worth not doing them.

There are companies that actually provide guidelines to employees on proper handshake etiquette. They talk about the origin of the handshake—that people extended their hand in ancient times to show the other person they didn't have a weapon in it—like that's a realistic scenario in corporate America today. (Actually, maybe it is.) It has since evolved as a gesture of goodwill, friendliness, sincerity, and affection. It has served as an unwritten bond to seal deals between two parties in lieu of written agreements.

I realize different cultures have different greetings, but they all have greetings of some kind. I'm just saying I don't like our handshake greeting—the act itself or how expected it is of us. Look, the only person I really want to have physical contact with is my wife. I have no desire to touch anyone else and I wouldn't expect them to want me to. So why do we have to do it?

Of course, when it comes to faking it, most people can't hide their true stripes forever. It soon becomes apparent who likes who, who is the department naysayer, who kisses up to the boss, who are the rebels, who is naïve, and who isn't the sharpest knife in the drawer. You can't really fake this stuff long term.

Nonetheless, a certain amount of fakery is necessary to survive in today's business world. It shouldn't be, but it is—like most Corporate Crap.

CHAPTER

13

Lunch

Bon appétit

I'd say we're ready for a lunch break. At least I am. When I worked in an office environment, I was always starving by the time it was acceptable to "take lunch." This was because as a morning person I would get to work by 7 a.m. when the rest of the world started at nine. I don't eat breakfast so I'd have to wait until at least eleven, when the cafeteria opened, so I could eat without people looking at me funny.

Of the many sources of stress we must deal with at work, lunch should not be one of them. Yet, for many of us, the company cafeteria, lunch room, break area, broom closet—wherever we are expected to eat lunch each day—is a place we dread. It goes beyond the normal issues of food quality, choice, cleanliness, or even the incredible number of people who walk up to us while we're in the middle of a two-fisted tuna sandwich wanting to shake hands. Of all the areas of Corporate Crap, lunchtime is one that causes many of us to lose our appetites.

Of course, lunch breaks among American workers vary considerably based on numerous factors. If you work nights, your "lunch" might actually be dinner or breakfast. If you work construction, it might be a lunch pail or trip to the nearest fast-food joint. If you work retail, you might frequent the mall's food court. This chapter deals primarily with lunchtime in office settings, which can range from no food options whatsoever to cafeterias with tablecloths and gourmet cuisine.

When I was in the corporate world, the worst thing about lunch was the mental baggage that comes with it. Deciding who to have lunch with can stir up anxiety not unlike that conjured up when asking someone out on a date. *If I ask Sue if she wants to have lunch, will she get the wrong idea? Should I also invite Debbie? Will Mark be pissed if we don't ask him to join us? Should we go out? Where should we go?*

The waste of mental energy is draining. Perhaps this is one reason less than 20 percent of American workers take a regular lunch break, according to a recent study. Another reason is that in today's competitive environment, some people feel like they can't afford to take lunch for fear of looking lazy compared to all the people who eat lunch at their desks or skip it entirely each day. Others skip lunch or eat at their desks because they have no other options.

On-site cafeterias, while not alleviating all of these issues, certainly make lunch easier to take and provide benefits to employers and employees. For employers, they reduce the amount of time employees take for lunch, which increases productivity. A study of Silicon Valley firms by management consultant Towers Watson found that having an on-site cafeteria saved between thirty and sixty minutes at lunchtime compared to going out. For employees, the cost of most cafeteria meals is less than restaurant or even fast-food meals, with employers often subsidizing meals for their employees as a perk.

There is some evidence that cafeterias can improve employee morale. The jobs website Glassdoor.com rated the best cafeterias in corporate America along with employee morale at these companies. At some companies, including

Google and Facebook, having very high-end food options for employees did indeed correlate to high employee satisfaction.

"I've forgotten how to make my own lunch," gushed one Google software engineer. A Facebook employee in Palo Alto, California, called the food in her cafeteria "amazing. We get breakfast, lunch, snack, and dinner served up by the best chefs around."

At companies such as Zynga, Marvel Technology, and Bloomberg L.P., however, employee morale was rated no better than "okay" despite cafeterias featuring free snacks, pizza, beer, and continental breakfast served daily. This makes the point that satisfaction depends on more than just a great cafeteria.

Most companies with cafeterias contract out the food service operation, although some employ their own chefs. The highest rated cafeterias feature healthy and often free food to employees, including exotic items like organic produce and grass-fed beef. Dishes include sushi, duck confit, braised salmon in coconut milk, beefsteak bordelaise, and beet-marinated tofu.

Some companies that don't have on-site food service operations cater lunch in for employees. "The catered lunches are a nice perk," says an employee for TripAdvisor. "They remove one thing to worry about." This supports my original thought: that the stress of having to make lunch plans each day is the worst part of lunch in corporate America.

Despite the apparent advantages of on-site cafeterias, less than 20 percent of companies have them, according to the Society for Human Resource Management. Not surprisingly, those that do are mostly large companies. Only about 10 percent of companies with fewer than 100 employees have cafeterias. Of course, some office buildings that house multiple tenants have shared cafeterias, so you could work for a very small company and still have access to a cafeteria.

"Nearly every company, even small ones, should have a cafeteria," says one management consultant. "People behave differently in a cafeteria. It becomes a gathering place for employees, increasing interaction and camaraderie."

The Towers Watson study cited earlier found that employees with access to a cafeteria were "more engaged" than employees without one. No, this does not mean cafeterias induce marriage. So what does it mean? Read on.

CHAPTER
14
Engagement

Would you marry your company?

Experts say you must have an engaged workforce to be an effective company. This is why companies spend zillions of dollars and countless man-hours on employee engagement surveys. We know companies don't like to throw money around based on how generous they are in compensating their rank and file. So they must really believe engagement surveys are critical to their success.

I never heard of engagement surveys when I started working. There were employee satisfaction surveys, I suppose, but this stuff wasn't nearly as scientific as it is today. Of course, there were no personal computers or Internet when I started working either. So I did some research, and it seems that engagement—loosely defined as how well you like your job—really does improve productivity. This is quite a revelation, that if employees like their jobs they'll do better, so companies invest in these surveys to see how well employees like their jobs.

When I took these surveys later in my career, they ignited in me the same urge to vent that exit interviews did. I could never seem to restrain myself whenever I was given the opportunity to lash out. Of course, this probably meant I wasn't as engaged as I should have been, so maybe these things do work.

Here are the top ten employee engagement survey questions, as determined by yet another survey, this one of HR professionals:

- How do you feel about coming to work every morning?
- Does your manager inspire you?
- Do the days you DO want to come to work outnumber the days you DON'T want to come to work?
- Choose five words that best describe how you feel about coming to work.
- Do you feel proud to tell people where you work?
- Do you have the tools to enable you to do your job effectively?
- Do you have the opportunity to contribute to decisions that affect you?
- Do you understand how your role contributes to achieving business outcomes?
- Do you trust the information you receive?
- Do you feel valued for the work you do?

The survey is just the starting point. After those dollars and incalculable man-hours are spent, HR will often put together task forces to analyze the results and come up with action plans to address areas where engagement is weak. These task forces, made up mostly of people with no expertise in employee engagement, will meet regularly and brainstorm enough ideas to fill several flip charts. Secretaries will spend weeks trying to decipher them into PowerPoint slides for the next meeting. Nothing usually results from these undertakings. They generally die of their own weight before anything tangible changes.

Every company is different, of course, which makes engagement like virtually everything else in the corporate world—an inexact science. Google is routinely voted one of the "Fortune 100 Best Companies to Work For" because of the unique perks it provides employees, like nap pods and free food. But experts in engagement caution against too much reliance on perks because they put the focus on what employees can get from the organization rather than truly feeling engaged with the organization and its goals.

What the company does for a living—the business it is in—can drive engagement. I worked for a number of companies in the health-care industry. Some of them made life-saving products. It seemed easier to feel proud to work for these companies than if I was working for a shoelace manufacturer. But even a company that makes a commodity like shoelaces might be active in the community or do other things that can make employees proud.

HR and business consultants are happy to work with companies on complex strategies to improve employee engagement. They often start with more surveys that delve deeper into "engagement drivers" identified in the initial surveys, impediments to boosting engagement scores, tools for managers, channels for improvement, defining the company's purpose, and on and on. They diagnose a company's engagement strategies and apply metrics to measure improvement. I cannot imagine a company in the real world going through all this, but some do.

When you cut through the bullshit, employee engagement is something else that ultimately comes down to the quality of your boss. Kevin Sheridan, a Chicago-based expert on employee engagement, wrote a book on the subject with the snappy title, *Building a Magnetic Culture: How to Attract and Retain Top Talent to Create an Engaged, Productive Workforce.*

"You have to hire the right managers," he says. "We're hiring bodies. We're getting butts into seats as opposed to having an interview process that's an absolute gauntlet." What he is saying is, it would be better if managers could manage effectively without employee engagement surveys.

Simply put, to have engaged employees, you have to hire high-caliber people for supervisory positions. If your boss treats you with respect, is open and honest, and acts personally and professionally secure, chances are you'll like your job more and thus be more engaged. All the rest is Corporate Crap.

CHAPTER
15
Myers & Briggs

Introverts vs. Extroverts

Speaking of useless surveys, what is with all of this introvert/
extrovert stuff? Suddenly it seems every company in America needs
to know which employees are introverts and which are extroverts—
as if you couldn't already tell. But now companies feel compelled
to do an official assessment of people's behavioral characteristics,
assign them to categories, and share the information with the rest
of the organization—purportedly to improve performance.

The folks who push this shit on organizations claim that
understanding the differences between introverts and extroverts can
help everyone get along better and thus perform better. Managers
can use the information to more effectively assemble and manage
teams with different personality types. You can use it to configure
office space, giving introverts more privacy, for example.

In the real world, most companies don't change anything
as a result of these tests. If you know that introverts prefer less
interaction than extroverts, you might manage them differently.
But good managers already do this without needing to know who
has officially been labeled an introvert or extrovert. They recognize
different tendencies in people and manage diverse personality types
differently.

I never would have guessed that out of all the topics for which
I solicited input for this book, the Myers-Briggs survey, used by

companies to assess levels of extraversion and introversion among employees, would elicit the most feedback. Everyone, it seems, has gone through this. Most employees reported it to be a waste of time. To others, like me, the sharing of results felt almost like an invasion of privacy. Other employees said they took the survey, but their company did not share the results.

"We had to line up from most extroverted to most introverted," says Erin, an account executive for a large public relations firm. "As the most extroverted, I didn't mind."

"We were sent to different corners of the room so we could see who's who," says Kelly, leader of a team responsible for upgrading medical software in hospitals. "It was a complete waste of time."

At the company where I did Myers-Briggs, everyone in the department was assigned to one of four categories based on what type of introvert or extrovert we were. We discussed the results at a staff meeting. All it did was let everyone know which box everyone fell into, labeling each person forever. Before the test I never thought of my coworkers in terms of who was an extrovert and who was an introvert. Now I did. Nothing else changed.

It reminded me of a diversity awareness workshop I participated in during the mid- to late-1980s. Companies were starting to do diversity awareness training to show their commitment to diversity and inclusion. In one exercise, people had to go to one side of the room or the other based on whether or not they believed in God, abortion rights, gay unions (gay marriage was unheard of back then), and other personal beliefs. Did I really need to know where all my colleagues stood on these issues? Did I like the fact that they now all knew where I stood? Did anything else change? The answer is "no" on all counts.

People form an identity around these labels. After Myers-Briggs it was as if each of my coworkers had "introvert" or "extrovert" branded on their forehead. I don't believe any of this improves relationships in the workplace. In fact, I believe these kinds of dynamics have the opposite effect.

The Myers-Briggs assessment is based on teachings that began with Swiss psychiatrist Carl Jung in the early twentieth century. Jung used the terms "extraversion" and "introversion" to explain how different motivating factors affect how people direct their energy. He defined introversion as "inwardly directed psychic energy." Introverts recharge by being alone. They lose energy when they're around other people. Extroverts gain energy from being social. They recharge by being with other people. They lose energy being alone.

Labeling employees introverts or extroverts implies that everyone belongs to one camp or the other. But Jung actually defined these terms as extremes on a scale of human behavior. "There is no such thing as a pure introvert or extrovert," Jung said. "Such a person would be in the lunatic asylum."

I find this scary because I seem to have all the characteristics of a pure introvert. But we may not know ourselves as well as we think. Our self-assessments are not always in line with how others see us. One interesting phenomenon I've noticed is that many extroverts seem to think they have more in common with introverts than their Myers-Briggs scores would indicate. "I know I seem like an extrovert, but I really am an introvert by nature" is a common refrain.

I think one reason for this is that introverts seem to be described in more complimentary terms than extroverts. The Myers & Briggs website provides a fairly balanced description: "Do you like to spend time in the outer world of people and things (extraversion) or in your inner world of ideas and imagination (introversion)?" But others make extroverts seem like bulls in a china shop compared to their more thoughtful and serene introverted colleagues. Extroverts are portrayed as impulsive: they talk before thinking, think out loud, and always have to be around other people. Introverts are described as more reflective: they like to work alone, think before they speak, and prefer one-on-one interactions.

Introverts are not necessarily shy. "Don't confuse introversion with shyness or reclusiveness," declares Myers & Briggs. "They are not related." Most social scientists agree. Shyness implies fear of social judgment. Most introverts simply find it tiring to be around other people.

Researchers have found differences in the brains of introverts and extroverts in terms of how much dopamine is released in response to different stimuli. Extroverts are turned on by "social attention often linked to money, power, and personal alliances." Introverts' brain scans show them to be less energized by such rewards versus things like quiet solitude and deep thought.

Extroverts who wish they were more like introverts should be careful what they wish for. There is a pretty strong bias toward extroverts in our culture and in the workplace. While introverts make up one-third to one-half of the population, "most workplaces are set up exclusively with extroverts in mind," according to a study in *Harvard Business Review*. Being enthusiastic, aggressive, and bold is celebrated in our society. A University of North Carolina study found that 96 percent of managers and executives display extroverted characteristics.

Does this make extroverts better leaders? That depends. A study published in the *Journal of Organizational Behavior* noted that "extroverts tend to be an energizing force in an already agreeable group. However, when there is a lot of disagreement, extroverts tend to cause more conflict. They are often seen as sharing their opinions in a domineering and aggressive manner." This research suggests that extroverted leadership may drive higher performance when employees are passive but lower performance when employees are proactive.

A more recent study from researchers at the University of Chicago, Harvard, and Stanford University found that introverted chief executives make better leaders.

"Extroverted leaders are more likely to feel threatened. When employees champion new visions, strategies, and work processes, they often steal the spotlight. Extroverted leaders tend to be less receptive to new ideas. By comparison introverted leaders are comfortable listening and carefully considering suggestions from below."

Going back to Jung's assertion that no one is a pure introvert or extrovert and that most of us fall somewhere in the middle, it follows that most of us are actually "ambiverts." So it should not be surprising that a 2013 study published in *Psychological Science* found the best performing employees are ambiverts. You need to be able to adapt across a spectrum of behavior to be successful no matter what your business. You need to be able to bend.

Of course, who knows how accurate any of this research is when the research also shows extroverts answer survey questions more enthusiastically than introverts. But the need to adapt to one's environment can't be denied. Just because Myers & Briggs labeled you an extrovert doesn't give you license to be a bully, rude, or an ass. Being declared an introvert doesn't mean you can skip meetings or go off on your own just because you don't want to have to deal with people. We all must adjust to the circumstances in which we find ourselves.

Which leads to the final point: How does knowing all this help companies? Why are they all investing in this? My friends at Second City Works have fairly strong opinions on Myers–Briggs.

"I was a cognitive science major in school," says Steve Kakos, vice president at Second City Works. "I was steeped in this shit. I am very anti–Myers–Briggs. It has no predictive validity at all. It's not science. It's based on artificial constructs that put people in boxes and doesn't mean anything. And organizations almost without fail will stereotype and act with prejudice against people who are introverts. In fact, it only makes introverts more introverted. There's actually science on that. And most of us are ambiverts, so what's the point?"

What's the point? There is no point. It's just Corporate Crap.

16

Brainstorming

Putting the storm before the brain

Nothing strikes fear and loathing into the hearts of employees—especially introverted employees—like the mass brainstorm session. A company's false sense of the creative process manifests itself in these amateur hours. It is based on the mistaken belief that the more uncensored garbage you can put on a flip chart, the better your chances of coming up with some groundbreaking idea—in other words, putting the storm before the brain.

"When it comes to brainstorming, we pretty much have one option: get everyone in a room and start throwing ideas out there," say authors Judah Pollack and Olivia Fox Cabane in an article in *Fast Company*. "This generally works well for the extroverts (though some say otherwise) and not so great for everyone else."

Actually, it doesn't work well for anyone if the goal is to come up with the best or even the most ideas. Most of us aren't very good at "free association" or coming up with ideas off the tops of our heads. And when we do free associate, studies show this technique tends to yield the most shallow, obvious, and predictable results rather than unique or "creative" ideas.

Worse is the mantra that "no idea is a bad idea." This not only is untrue and inane, it actually does the opposite of what it is supposed to do, which is free people from censoring themselves for fear of being criticized. The assumption is that if people are afraid their idea might be criticized, they will shut down and not contribute. In reality, the dynamics of the freewheeling idea-dump do more to inhibit the best ideas from emerging than fear of being criticized. In fact, criticism has been shown to be vital to coming up with the best solutions to problems.

The roots of the brainstorm session as we know it go back to 1948 when a Madison Avenue advertising executive named Alex Osborn published a book called *Your Creative Power*. He defined the "brainstorm" as "using the brain to storm a creative problem—and doing so in commando fashion, with each 'stormer' attacking the same objective." The key to unlocking people's creativity, he said, was freeing them from the constraints of negative feedback.

"Creativity is so delicate a flower that praise tends to make it bloom while discouragement often nips it in the bud," he said. "Forget quality; aim for quantity."

But if most of the ideas are impractical due to time, staff, or budget constraints and are just thrown up there because "no idea is a bad idea," what good are they? Is this really the best way to solve a specific problem or issue, which is what most brainstorming sessions seek to do?

Charlan Nemeth, a professor of psychology at the University of California-Berkeley, is a critic of the "no idea is a bad idea" philosophy. Her studies show it to be counterproductive in generating usable ideas.

"Our findings show that debate and criticism do not inhibit ideas but, rather, stimulate them. There's this Pollyannaish notion that the most important thing to do when working together is stay positive and get along, to not hurt anyone's feelings. That's just wrong. Maybe debate is going to be less pleasant, but it will always be more productive. True creativity requires some tradeoffs. Authentic dissent can be difficult, but it's always invigorating. It wakes us up."

This idea of having to protect fragile egos from criticism reminds me of how they coach Little League baseball today. It's all about positive reinforcement. "Good try, Billy!" when he lets a ball go through his legs. When I played Little League, the coach would have yelled, "Harrison, get your head out of your ass!" This actually happened once when I got picked off third base. It was embarrassing but it taught me to pay attention when you're on the bases like you're supposed to. Today they're afraid yelling at a kid will scar him or her for life.

Decades of research also have shown that group brainstorming sessions yield fewer ideas than when people work alone and pool their ideas. The first study refuting Osborn's theories on brainstorming was in 1958 at Yale University. Study groups were instructed to brainstorm freely without criticism to come up with solutions to a series of puzzles, while control groups were told to work alone. The students working alone came up with twice as many solutions as the brainstorming groups. Their solutions also were deemed more "feasible" and "effective." Brainstorming, rather than unleashing each person's creativity, made each person less creative. Most studies since have produced similar results.

I have an idea. How about putting the brain before the storm? Let people think on their own first. Let them submit ideas individually or in groups, interact with each other or not, give their brains time for self-assessment or feedback if they'd like. I'm just saying there are other ways to get ideas and solve problems than the free-for-all that masquerades as creativity in organizations.

Writing out your ideas beforehand has other benefits. How often does someone say after a brainstorm session, "I thought of that but didn't say it because I didn't think it was what you were looking for"? Or you run out of time in these sessions? Writing out your ideas beforehand eliminates these issues.

Writing your ideas in longhand rather than typing them on your iPad or keyboard also might be beneficial. I recommend you try it. I was taught this when I took comedy writing classes at Second City way back in the day. They had us write our sketches longhand because supposedly your brain works differently than when you type at a keyboard. They said you're more creative. I have found some merit in this as a writer. But whether you use longhand or keyboard, there is something to be said for thinking first versus spewing ideas off the cuff.

"Almost everybody does brainstorming wrong," says Ralph Keeney, emeritus professor at Duke University's Fuqua School of Business. He published a book called *Value-Focused Thinking: A Path to Creative Decision-Making* in which he supports my assertion that companies tend to put the storm before the brain when it comes to brainstorming. "When most people do brainstorming, they run all over the place to think outside the box. They should think inside the box."

Most employees are best thinking "in the box." The evidence shows the best ideas come from situations where the scope of thinking is at least somewhat constrained. Without some guidance, people can get frustrated and shut down. Again, most people just aren't good at unstructured, abstract brainstorming. Solving problems requires focused thought, not darts thrown randomly at a wall.

Companies also ignore the human dynamics that inevitably take over in these settings. Obviously, the people who get their adrenaline rush from being the most vocal contributor in the room completely shut down those who are more reserved. The first ideas presented also tend to get undue time and attention.

Some experts suggest using a facilitator to maintain some balance, someone who can call upon those not speaking up to give them a chance to contribute. But how does the facilitator know if that person is sitting on an idea or simply doesn't have anything to contribute? You run the risk of embarrassing that person, like in school when the teacher would suddenly without warning say something like, "Howard, we haven't heard from you yet. What do you have to say?" God, I hated that.

As someone who is most effective working alone, one on one, or in very small groups, I am averse to mass brainstorm sessions. The cliché about too many cooks seems to apply. I believe talented individuals drive success. It doesn't mean they can't or shouldn't work together. But these mass idea exchanges and overreliance on democracy diffuse what's good and bad, and there will always be people not satisfied with the group decision. It's just more Corporate Crap.

17

Corporate Jargon

Alphabet Soup

"Okay, before we get started, does anyone have a hard stop?"
I was taken aback. It was our first staff meeting with our new boss.
I didn't know what she was asking. It sounded kind of personal. I
soon learned it means a non-negotiable time by which you must
leave the meeting. Instead of saying, "Before we get started, does
anyone have to leave early?" you say, "Before we get started, does
anyone have a hard stop?"

I guess it's a little shorter. It still sounds like you're asking about
someone's bowel movements, at least to me, but that's not the point.
The point is that corporate America has its own lexicon of jargon.
My new boss really had it down, a walking encyclopedia of the
latest corporate clichés. What I'd like to know is how these phrases
get started and then proliferate like wildfire across every industry.

The first time I heard the phrase "at the end of the day"
was in 1985. I worked in employee communications for Baxter
Healthcare, which had just agreed to acquire American Hospital
Supply Corporation, creating the largest vertically integrated health
care products company in the industry. I was interviewing one of
American's executives about his business. As he was about to sum
up, he said, "So at the end of the day ..." and then summarized his
main points. I'd never heard this expression before. I kind of liked
it. It had a rolled-up shirtsleeves feel to it. It reminded me of the

release you feel "at the end of the day" right before you go home, crack open a beer, and decompress.

The first time I heard "bandwidth" was 1994. I'd just gone into business for myself, and a client asked if I had enough "bandwidth" to take on a project. She meant capacity. Back then when I thought of "bandwidth," I thought of the dial on a transistor radio. Soon another client used "bandwidth." Before long everyone was using it to describe someone's availability. "Sorry but I have a lot on my plate," I might answer. (It's okay to mix metaphors in the world of corporate jargon.) The word "capacity" today is used more to refer to physical inventory space.

You could write entire books on corporate jargon. Some people have. Other favorites of mine when I worked in corporate America were *win-win, net-net, in the sandbox, leverage, utilize* (why not *use?*), *synergy, value add, blue sky, touch base, move the needle, tee it up,* and *the view from 30,000 feet.*

I don't know if people still use those as much. I'm sure there are many new buzzwords I'm not familiar with. The thing about corporate jargon is that some words and phrases get used so much they become clichés after a while. At that point, anyone with any self-awareness will stop using these terms for fear of embarrassing themselves by becoming a live parody of corporate bullshit.

"Their credibility actually goes down because people wonder, 'Why can't you just use normal words?'" says James Sudakow, author of the book *Picking the Low-Hanging Fruit ... and Other Stupid Stuff We Say in the Corporate World.* Sudakow, who runs a management consulting firm in California, says people in the corporate world use jargon because it allows them "to look like they're part of a special group that knows what this stuff means."

Any discussion of corporate jargon must include companies' obsession with acronyms. It borders on psychotic. We're not just talking *ASAP, FYI,* and so on. We're talking corporate slogans where the first letter of each word spells out some larger word of all-encompassing importance. We're talking acronyms for all the committees companies put together to do whatever it is they do. We're talking acronyms for how you do business (B2B, B2C), titles (CEO, COO, CFO, CIO, CSO), financial indicators (EBITDA, ROI), business functions (QC, PR, R&D), business processes (SEO, IPO, RFP), and for a slew of other business terms.

At many companies, the Senior Leadership Team would be referred to internally as the SLT. If the company name is ACME (itself an acronym), it might be the ACME Leadership Team or the ALT. If you work for Baxter, however, you can't really have a Baxter Leadership Team, or BLT, because it sounds like a sandwich and people would make fun of it. So instead you might have the Baxter Leadership Committee, or BLC. The company's Finance department might have a Finance Leadership Committee (FLC) and so on.

For people like my boss in the beginning of this chapter, these acronyms become a second language, or even a first language. When acronyms are coupled with corporate jargon, you really need a translator. I can't tell you how many times I had no idea what in the name of Roget this woman was talking about:

"FYI, the HRLC is meeting in BL2 to discuss the ROI on SPIN based on the KPI from the FLC. The GMT will decide to issue RFPs for an ISP that the SLT can approve by Q1. Talk to the CIO and CTO to see net-net how to position with the BLC. It should be a win–win because it leverages SEO with HTML, providing synergies that add value to the VPN. They'll determine the RRP. Let me know your ETA by EOD."

If you couldn't figure that out, you couldn't have worked for this woman. If you could figure it out, I feel bad for you. You clearly need a vacation.

CHAPTER
18
Time Off

Yours, Mine, and Hours

More than half of American workers don't take all their vacation days. More than 700 million vacation days went unused in 2017. This is affecting people's health. Research shows the more people work, the greater the risk of heart disease, cancer, diabetes, and other conditions. It's also bad for business. Statistics show that people who take vacations are more productive workers. Not taking vacations also costs the economy hundreds of billions of dollars a year in lost revenue. So why aren't people taking vacations? What is wrong with you people?

Pardon me for being obvious, but there are only seven days in a week. Most people already devote at least five to work. There are fifty-two weeks in a year. The average company gives you two for vacation. How can you not relish such scarce free time, even if you love your job, which most people don't?

The Project Time Off Coalition—a group backed by the travel industry—cites work pressures as the main reason employees don't take vacation time. They are afraid that taking vacation makes them appear less dedicated and indispensable to the company. I get it. It's the competitive culture we are in. The same people who don't take lunch tend to have desk surfaces that haven't seen the light of day in years, and never leave before the boss, all to show everyone how goddamn busy they are. But come on, folks. Relinquish your vacation days?

Asking for and negotiating time off has been an indignity of corporate life for a long time. But you should not feel guilty if your job is not the most important thing in your life. And again, the benefits of time off aren't all one-sided. There are bills in Congress designed to encourage employers to offer more time off in the way of vacation and sick days, as well as more flexible work arrangements, to employees.

The root of the problem is Corporate America's obsessive focus on hours, clocks, and time schedules as opposed to things like talent, performance, or results. It's easier to manage this way. It's easier to maintain control, assess compliance, know where everyone is, and keep everyone honest. Yet the nine-to-five workday is irrelevant to nearly half the workforce. According to the U.S. Bureau of Labor Statistics, 42 percent of us do not work at a job where "being there" at a specific time is necessary to do the job.

This is not the case, of course, at businesses where you need employees to work specific shifts, such as retail establishments or manufacturing plants. But for the rest of the workforce, the hours you work should be meaningless if you do what you're being paid to do and meet all of your responsibilities.

"Our culture in the U.S. is rooted in what I call an hours mentality," says a human resources consultant with Aon-Hewitt. Even alternatives to the traditional nine-to-five, like the four-day workweek, are still hours-based. And if an alternative is hours-based, people feel like they need to be seen putting in more hours to score points. "To make an impression, you want to be the first person in and the last one out."

I agree with the last part, that people like to be seen working late. But no one is there to see the first one in. I know because that was usually me. I work best when it's still dark outside and most people are still sleeping. At my last corporate job I usually got to the office several hours before anyone else. All anyone saw, however, was me leaving at four while they all stayed till six or later.

Most companies aren't mature enough (and to be honest, neither are most employees) to let people just do their jobs, keep their own hours, and be assessed solely on the basis of their work. But it would do them and their people well if they could at least acknowledge that not everyone shares the same biorhythms or works their best at the same time of day and allow more flexibility.

"The last thing (employees) want to do is work for a company with rigid schedules, where they're expected to be in a cubicle from nine to five," says Lisa Horn, head of the Society of Human Resources Management (SHRM). In the group's 2017 Employee Satisfaction and Engagement Report, the SHRM cited flexibility as "very important" to employees' job satisfaction.

Since 1970, the number of households with two working parents has risen 50 percent. Yet despite the increased work/life challenges this presents, most companies have not changed their workplace structures. Much of this is due to employers' lack of trust that employees won't abuse more flexible arrangements.

While you'd expect employee satisfaction to increase if employees could pick their own hours, the question is, would work output suffer? In a recent study, for a six-month period, 500 employees of one Fortune 500 company were allowed to set their own hours based on what worked best for them.

During this time, they also attended workshops provided by the company designed to help them manage their time under these new conditions. Lo and behold, at the end of six months, employee satisfaction increased and the quality of work did not suffer. Personally, I think they could have attained this result without the workshops.

AT&T Mobility's attendance policy was the cause of a class-action lawsuit claiming discrimination against pregnant women. The company's point-based system assigned demerits if employees were late, absent, or left early for any reason other than jury duty or short-term disability. At least two pregnant women were fired for missing too much time due to pregnancy-related medical care.

"They treat employees like cogs, but employees aren't cogs," said one of the attorneys in the lawsuit. "They're human. They get pregnant. They get sick. They have families that need to be taken care of."

Companies would do themselves a favor by lightening up on their "hours-based" mentality. Perhaps legal issues like this one will get their attention. Lawsuits have a way of doing that, especially when it comes to firing people.

CHAPTER
19
Firing People

You don't need a reason. Just do it.

In today's litigious society companies have become more uneasy about firing people. They're reluctant to fire someone just because "it's not working out" even though legally most can do so. Instead they develop performance improvement plans, provide coaching and feedback, document the employee's progress (or lack thereof), and embark on a prolonged series of verbal warnings, written warnings, and come-to-Jesus meetings before finally pulling the plug.

Companies use a variety of terms to tell you you're fired. They usually don't say "fired." More often you are being laid off, terminated, dismissed, displaced, or "let go." One company I worked for used the term "impacted" to describe employees who lost their jobs. Or they say your job is being eliminated, which is often just an excuse to get rid of someone.

There are legal reasons—as in fear of being sued—for companies to tread lightly on how and why they fire people. But for the most part, companies are more cautious than they need to be. The fact is that legally most employers do not need a reason to fire you. It is totally legal to fire someone without cause. Unless you have a contract or work under a collective bargaining agreement that states otherwise, most employees in the United States work "at will," meaning your employer doesn't need a reason to fire you.

In fact, it is when employers *do* state a reason, or cause, that they open themselves up to lawsuits. For example, if they say they're firing you because of performance and your performance is no worse than someone else's who is not being fired, you could claim discrimination. It is illegal to fire someone because of race, gender, national origin, disability, religion, genetics, or age. Many states also prohibit discrimination on the basis of sexual orientation and marital status.

You can't fire someone for not taking a lie detector test because of the federal Employee Polygraph Protection Act. There are laws against firing someone because they threaten to blow the whistle on suspected wrongdoing by the company. So really, you're better off not stating a cause.

What if one of your employees is a white supremacist? Can they be fired for that?

In 2017, white nationalists marched in Charlottesville, Virginia. Photos of some of them were posted on social media. They soon were identified and information about them was also posted, including where they worked. Some of their employers were pressured to fire these people. Some did.

Is it right to fire people because of their political beliefs? I don't know if it's right, but it's not illegal unless you work for the government. There is no federal law that specifically protects people from being fired for what they do outside of work, what views they hold, or how they express them. So, it's okay to fire people simply for being racist jerks. But it's even easier to fire people without cause.

There is a ton of literature on how and how not to fire people. Experts agree that taking away someone's livelihood warrants a face-to-face meeting. You should not fire people over the Internet or phone, or by mail, electronic or snail. The legendary "pink slip" is more myth than reality. Friday also is not necessarily the best day to fire someone. Some experts think it is, but others say it doesn't matter.

When firing someone face-to-face, some experts suggest the firing manager have another person in the room with them. This is not so much in case the employee flips out—although that would make sense to me—but to have a witness so the employee can't lie about what went down when you fired him or her.

And they tell you to keep a box of Kleenex handy. Really?

As I alluded to earlier, the biggest problem companies have in firing people is that they take too long. This is the overwhelming consensus of virtually all researchers and business consultants on this topic. "Firing is the single most difficult thing we ask leaders to do," says Dick Grote, author of *How to Be Good at Performance Appraisals* (Harvard Business Review Press).

Some managers find it so hard to fire people that they can't. They don't. They ride it out, make feeble attempts to change the employee, and live in constant stress until the situation finally becomes intolerable.

"The most common problem with terminations is that they don't happen as fast as they should," Grote says. "Once the decision has been made to pull the plug and start over, don't dilly-dally in the misguided hope that somehow things may still work out. They never do."

"There is nothing worse you can do for your organization than to continue to let a poorly performing team member linger," says one CEO. "As the leader of your organization, or a manager within it, it's your responsibility to make the decisions that will put the team and organization in the best position to succeed."

In other words, if a department would function better without someone, it is best to fire that person ASAP. Remember, you don't need a reason. Just do it.

CHAPTER
20
Teamwork

Corporate Team-Building

I apologize for using so many baseball analogies in this book, but I'm a fan and I can't help but relate some of the lessons from the National Pastime to the corporate world.

In Game 3 of Major League Baseball's 2017 National League divisional playoffs, series tied 1-1 and the game scoreless in the sixth inning, Chicago Cubs left fielder Kyle Schwarber dropped a ball that allowed the Washington Nationals to score the lead run. No one felt worse than Schwarber. But his teammates came to his defense, vowing to "pick him up," which they did, coming back to win the game.

Afterward, Cubs manager Joe Maddon was asked what he thought of his players rallying around Schwarber to make sure his mistake did not cost the Cubs the game. "Isn't that wonderful?" Maddon said. "Wouldn't you like that kind of camaraderie in your workplace?"

The reporters laughed, knowing how rare such selflessness is in most workplaces. Companies are different than baseball teams, of course, although I know a guy who wrote a book comparing successful teams in different industries to see what they had in common. He researched a diverse array of successful teams in recent history—sports teams, space crews, military squads, and others—and cited common traits that contributed to their success.

The book sold a lot of copies and the guy made quite a name for himself on the lecture circuit. He was kind of a gregarious, ego-driven guy who loved performing, loved the spotlight, loved being up there preaching to executives about teamwork. He had his script down, using the same anecdotes and jokes each performance like he was doing Vegas. It catapulted him to great success. He became a corporate officer for a large health-care company—not bad for someone who until then had been a mid-level HR manager most of his career.

A few years later I was at a seminar on teamwork. The moderator was familiar with the guy I knew and his book on teamwork. "Funny thing about Frank," he said to me. "He's Mister Teamwork, right? Have you ever been on a team with Frank?" I thought for a moment. I'd worked with Frank but was never on a "team" with him. "It's his way or the highway. Frank is not a team player." I liked Frank. But I could see what this guy was saying. Frank did seem to have a high opinion of himself and often acted like he thought he was superior to everyone else.

As for his book, I doubt it had much impact in helping companies improve teamwork in their own organizations. It did make some interesting observations, though. One common trait of successful teams, according to the book, is having "a clear and elevating goal." Another is trust. I found the well-substantiated "trust curve" particularly interesting. It showed that if someone breaks your trust just once, you will never fully trust that person again. It is a powerful demonstration of how hard it is to regain trust once you lose it.

"Trust is critical in business because it can make or break a team, and business can no longer survive without teams," says one Fortune 500 CEO.

I agree trust is critical. I'm not sure a business can't survive without teams. But the only way to earn trust is to be trustworthy. If you are and always have shown yourself to be honest, then people will trust you. Can you teach trustworthiness? I don't think so. But there are plenty of companies that try to foster teamwork through "team-building" exercises designed to bring people closer together and develop trust in one another.

Some of these exercises are fairly benign, like having employees stare into each other's eyes for more than a minute without looking away, or sharing personal information about themselves. Other team-building exercises include things like trust falls (closing your eyes and falling backward into the arms of a colleague), escape rooms (analogous to prisoners conspiring a jailbreak), or making people zip-line across valleys in tandem to build trust and get over fears.

Some team-building exercises have employees work together to solve hypothetical business problems. These exercises are generally presented in a workshop setting with facilitators providing guidance along the way, such as the importance of everyone participating, not placing blame, and other lessons. My friends at Second City Works provide team-building workshops that apply principles of improvisational comedy. Some companies will plan group charitable events that double as team-building activities, such as employees working together on a house for Habitat for Humanity.

The results of these activities on teamwork in these organizations are hard to quantify. Organizational psychologists question whether they have any tangible effect at all on performance. "Anything that requires people to work together, think critically, and solve a problem is going to have more of a benefit than just standing in a forest and falling backwards and having everyone catch you," says one. "So some team-building activities are better than others."

Then there are outings that simply provide some group entertainment or get employees out of the office together. Some companies may categorize these under "team-building" to justify the expense, but that's a stretch. I don't want to come off as Mr. Corporate Curmudgeon, but are things like sporting events, dinner cruises, retreats, golf outings, entertainers, and so on really going to help your people work better together?

"It's not clear yet what are the benefits of these outings other than employees love them because it's something outside of work," says an organizational psychology professor at Rice University. "But when they go back, the same conditions are there, so the long-term effects on team-building are unknown."

There is nothing wrong with using social activities to reward employees or break up the monotony of the office. Let's just not make more of this than it is. If you want to call them "team-building exercises," fine. They're not boondoggles as long as you have fun. We need to have more fun in our jobs. Hey, let's party!

CHAPTER
21
Office Parties

Who Wants to Party?

In my first book—*NOW They Make It Legal: Reflections of an Aging Baby Boomer*—there was a chapter titled "Party: The Verb." I explained how we Baby Boomers took a noun "used to describe an event where people get together to celebrate or have a good time" and turned it into a verb that means "to get high, drunk, stoned, or somehow inebriated, usually with others."

Increasingly, companies are trying to eliminate partying, the verb, from office parties and other business gatherings because, frankly, they can't trust people's behavior when they get tipsy. Specifically, they are cutting down on the open bars where unlimited access to alcohol has historically offered comic relief at stuffy business functions.

Alcohol is the legal, sanctioned drug of our society. While virtually all other mood-altering substances are frowned upon, alcohol is glorified for helping us to celebrate virtually anything as well as drown our sorrows when things are bad. It also can make you act like a jerk, say things you'll regret, and get your company in trouble. Companies no longer want to risk the legal liabilities.

Office parties that are held on-site in the afternoon such as employee birthday and anniversary parties generally don't feature alcohol. Of course, that's in the United States. "In Europe, alcohol at lunch is normal," says Gabriel, who works in France. "A birthday party in the office with a glass of champagne is nice."

It sounds nice, although some of us in the States might fall asleep at our desks afterward. For most U.S. employees, the company event most likely to include alcohol has always been the annual Christmas party. Nowadays these are usually called "holiday" parties to sound more inclusive.

Whatever you call them, these events bring introverts and extroverts together to celebrate the end of the year. You'd think the extroverts would be thrilled and the introverts would look for the nearest foxhole, but this is not always the case, especially if there's alcohol involved. I'm an introvert and I used to love business functions with an open bar. This was probably because once the alcohol kicked in, I was no longer an introvert. Alcohol has a way of doing that to some people.

"Over 40 percent of employees report having seen or experienced embarrassing holiday party conduct" when alcohol was served, according to one law firm in a warning to companies on the perils of serving alcohol at their holiday parties. The firm called office parties in general "fertile ground" for lawsuits.

Companies have been throwing fewer holiday parties since 2010, when recession forced many to cancel or cut down on their celebrations for economic reasons. Gone for many were the professionally catered affairs with lavish hors d'oeuvres, hand-carved filet, and fancy ice sculptures. Since then, most of the downturn has been due to worries about legal liability driven by the presence of alcohol. In 2017, a surge of high-profile sexual harassment cases provided another reason.

With or without alcohol, company parties present challenges for employers and employees. Fortunately, as with every aspect of corporate life, there are consultants out there to help. Career counselors encourage employees to view company social events as opportunities to boost their livelihoods by broadening their scope of business contacts. "Once an hour, try to meet someone you don't know," says one such consultant. "I don't care what business you're in; the more people you have relationships with, the more it can benefit you."

There are consultants who teach employees how to properly conduct themselves at such gatherings—essentially how to schmooze. They provide tips on how to carry yourself, approach people, when it's okay to interrupt, when to offer a handshake. They teach you how to "start a conversation with flattery" and make eye contact. Some tell you to work the room with a "wingman" and prepare for the party by checking out the LinkedIn profiles of people who might be there.

There is specific advice on holiday parties, like commenting on the decorations or homemade treats that might be on the table, or asking people about their plans for the holidays. They remind you of proper phone etiquette and to make sure you don't come off like you're "brown-nosing" even though you are.

In addition to warning companies to watch it with the booze, consultants advise them on things like appropriate dress codes for employees at company events and what activities to avoid to reduce potential legal issues.

"I'm sure this information is valuable to people considering adding beer pong, wet T-shirt contests, or scripture readings to their holiday office parties," says Rex Huppke, whose witty sarcasm can be enjoyed daily in the Chicago Tribune. Rex used to write a column on workplace practices.

"It's another example of the way overly worried managers and outside experts infantilize the workplace," he says. "Most working people know that drinking to excess and barfing on the boss's shoes is a bad idea. Most know that bringing up religion in a social situation is unwise. I believe a company generally does more good when it errs on the side of respecting the intelligence of its employees."

The last holiday party I attended was my last day as a full-time employee in the corporate world. It was our department Christmas party, on-site in the afternoon, so there was no alcohol. There was food but the party mostly featured the gift exchange. I don't recall if it was a "secret Santa," "white elephant," or some other roundabout way to give someone a scented candle or receive a Santa Claus oven mitt. But I was in good spirits, despite no spirits, making fun of the lame gifts and jokingly accusing my coworker of putting marijuana in her spinach dip.

Immediately after the party, my boss and I sat down for our weekly one-on-one meeting. She and I had never seen eye to eye in the eighteen months since she joined the company and took over our department. Turns out I had interviewed her for an internship early in our careers and not hired her. She joked that she wouldn't hold it against me. I don't think she did, but she might have. As soon as we sat down after the Christmas party, she told me she was eliminating my position.

This, of course, was bullshit. She had my replacement all lined up, just with a slightly different title and job responsibilities. This was simply her way of getting her own person in there, and I totally understood. I even helped her save face by going along with the charade that I was leaving voluntarily, as I was fairly well-liked and respected by a lot of people in the organization, including the CEO.

That said, it's probably a good thing I wasn't liquored up. "Merry Christmas to you too," I said under my breath, followed by the most vulgar of sexist names. Then I went home and poured myself a scotch.

CHAPTER

22

Restructuring/Reengineering

Trimming the Fat

It's been called restructuring, reengineering, rightsizing, delayering, retooling, and other strategic language that ultimately means mass layoffs. It's even been called downsizing, although companies prefer not to use this term. In reality, which word a company uses depends on which one it deems least offensive in describing the need or desire to "trim the fat" and operate more efficiently.

I've been through a few of these. It often starts with a rumor that "consultants" are on-site poking around and meeting with senior management. This is followed by a lot of closed-door meetings and more whispered rumors. Ultimately a carefully crafted internal announcement goes out explaining how competition in the marketplace and other dynamics are forcing the company to rethink how it does things and find ways to improve efficiencies.

Companies often undertake these efforts after mergers and acquisitions to eliminate redundant positions and divest businesses that are no longer a strategic fit. When I worked at Baxter Healthcare, the company went through three restructurings between 1985 and 1994—one every three years—before finally settling down after its historic merger with American Hospital Supply Corporation.

At that time, U.S. businesses were merging, consolidating, and downsizing at a record pace in response to increased global competition and rapid technological change. More than two million middle-management positions were eliminated in corporations across America during this period. It marked the end of the unspoken contract between employers and employees for long-term employment and ushered in the so-called "lean" philosophy in American business.

When Baxter acquired American Hospital Supply in 1985—the merger became official in 1986—there were many redundant positions that had to be eliminated, particularly at the corporate level. I had to interview for my own job because American also had a manager of employee communications. I was lucky enough to keep my job. My counterpart from American and thousands of other employees from both premerger organizations lost theirs.

From a revenue standpoint, the company had doubled in size, combining Baxter's international leadership in select medical therapies with American's broad-based product line and distribution capabilities. But three years into the merger, the company still had not fully consolidated, and it was finding a newly cost-conscious global health-care marketplace more challenging than anticipated.

This time the company was not shy about declaring that it needed to undertake a major restructuring. I was involved in much of the communications that went out to employees but that didn't guarantee me anything. Each department had to cut heads. Our department would go from more than thirty people to less than half that.

When the day arrived, we were brought down to Human Resources in groups to learn our fate. If you came back upstairs, you made it. If you didn't, it meant they had already ushered you out of the building. Once again, I survived. I actually came out better. Baxter canned my boss and promoted me to Director of Internal Communication.

While the way the company informed employees was awkward, it was better than some companies do it.

"One of my previous companies announced that they were going to lay off a large percentage of employees due to bankruptcy," says Stephanie. "Everyone knew the day it was going to happen but nobody knew for sure who would be 'saved.' On the fated day, the mystery was solved as soon as people came in and logged onto their computer. The IT department shut down the email of all employees who were on the chopping block. So if you couldn't log in, you were gone."

By the time Baxter was ready for its next restructuring in 1994, I had had enough. I was thirty-eight and ready to go into business for myself. I went to the corporate VP and offered my head in exchange for a severance package. I was doing her a favor. She had to cut one head and I saved her the trouble. I left on good terms and Baxter became my biggest client. Eleven years later I rejoined the company, doing mostly executive communications, and stayed for another six years.

Corporate America has continued to downsize as technology makes it possible to eliminate more people. As I said earlier, companies don't like to call it downsizing because the word clearly means reducing the number of people the organization employs. "Workforce reduction" is even more direct. Some companies call it "rightsizing" but that, too, implies eliminating resources even though theoretically it can also mean "upsizing," i.e., increasing the workforce in certain areas.

Most companies prefer to use terms like "reengineering" or "restructuring" to disguise mass layoffs as efforts to change structures, systems, and/or processes. It still results in downsizing. It still results in mass layoffs. But the term itself does not necessarily imply a reduction in anything as much as a change in organization.

Some companies describe their restructuring efforts as a way to "flatten" the organization and push decision-making down to lower levels. By removing layers in the hierarchy, "we can be more responsive to customer needs," they say. Many companies use this to justify their restructuring efforts and make them sound like more than just getting rid of people. Some companies call it "decentralization."

If I were picking a term, I think I'd just call it all "rejiggering." That pretty much covers it, don't you think? All the rest is Corporate Crap.

CHAPTER
23
Development

Helping Us Grow

I feel I should wrap up this book with a look to the future. After all, a lot of companies seem to do this almost from the moment you're hired, or maybe even before. Screw the present. What's your potential? Where do you ultimately want to go in the company? Where do you see yourself in five years?

It's not that companies really care about you that much. They've simply been suckered into investing gobs of money in "training and development" because, as one major consulting firm asserts, "organizations with high-impact learning deliver profit growth three times greater than their competitors."

I don't know what "high-impact learning" is or how it's measured, but anything that can help produce three times greater profit growth is going to get companies' attention. And all the literature touts training and development as more important than ever in organizations today. It is said to help boost employee retention and business performance, and it is cited more than any other area in "best companies to work for" surveys.

It is also big business. Some companies have their own training and development functions, usually part of Human Resources. But even these companies are likely to go outside for sophisticated training and development programs complete with thick binders and manuals with hierarchical triangles and flowcharts, along with online courses.

First, let's distinguish between training and development, as they are not the same. Training is more immediate: providing employees with specific knowledge and skill-building to improve performance in their current job. Examples would be supervisory training for new managers, or ethics and compliance training for all employees. Development focuses on an employee's long-term professional growth.

I can see how advanced education in some fields is necessary to stay current, and why companies would provide this versus leaving it to employees to stay current on their own. In a survey by the Pew Research Center of more than 8,000 executives, hiring managers, college professors, and technology analysts, nearly a third of respondents said education and job training in the private sector are not adequate to meet the future labor needs of American businesses. This was not a knock on the education system as much as an acknowledgment that future labor needs are going to be much different than they are today.

One respondent, asked about the workforce of the future, said, "Seriously? As if there's going to be one?" Many respondents expect automation to continue to change or even eliminate the role of the human in the workplace. I will not get into this metaphysical discussion. "The next generation of workers should learn how to code," the report states. That's enough for me.

The thing about employee development that rankled me as an employee was the notion that if you are simply good at your job and don't want to do anything else, you are not valued. You must want to "grow"—even beyond your chosen field of expertise—or you are seen as unambitious.

I don't get this. If I have a business and need certain things done, and I have people who do those jobs exceedingly well and don't want to do anything else, why do I want to move those people out of those jobs? Why is this one of my "development goals"? Why do I have "development goals"? I'm looking at it from the bottom-line perspective of a businessman. Why should I have to worry about that shit?

It takes a while to realize one's potential in a chosen field. You enter college at the ripe old age of eighteen and come out seeking a job where you can put your degree to use. You are nowhere near the top of your game. You're just getting started. But ideally you eventually get real good at what you do and serve your employer well in that capacity for as long as they need that job done and you want to do it.

Sounds simple, right? But again, unfortunately, companies have to screw things up with more Corporate Crap. They believe they must be in the employee-development business in addition to the business they are actually in. They feel the need to develop you, to force you to continue to grow, no matter how good you may be in your current job and regardless of whether you care to ascend.

Do not confuse "development" with "opportunity" even though many companies blur the lines. For example, I had to work for several corporate communications VPs whose backgrounds were in law, human resources, or some other field than communications. These appointments were made in part as "executive development opportunities." In the meantime, these amateurs were calling shots in areas some of us actually had to go to school for, making poor decisions and driving everyone crazy—while receiving corporate officer-level pay to boot.

At Baxter, the only company for which I worked as a regular employee for more than two years, moving up ultimately meant doing less writing—what I liked to do and was very good at—and more "managing." If I had wanted to be a corporate executive, I'd have gotten an MBA instead of a journalism degree.

What put me over the edge was when I had to manage an outside writer on Baxter's annual shareholder report. I had previously written the report myself and won numerous awards. This was a $10 billion global company. It took a lot of hand-holding to manage this guy. I had to tell him what questions to ask in his interviews with management. Then I had to explain to him their answers. I had to rewrite his copy multiple times. The CEO insisted I write the Chairman's Letter. So, what did this guy do besides make more work, not less work, for me?

He made $35,000 on the project, that's what. Then when the book came out, he had the audacity to complain that his name wasn't listed as the copywriter. I told him he was lucky his name was on the check. Then I figured, if this no-talent nozzle-head can make $35,000 on one annual report—and do a shitty job no less—what could I make if I went out on my own? So I quit, became an independent contractor, and wrote Baxter's annual report from the outside for a number of years.

There are actually companies that are called Deliberately Developmental Organizations (DDOs). These organizations make no bones about being more devoted to employee development than they are to their present business.

"Their big bet on a deliberately developmental culture is rooted in the unshakable belief that business can be an ideal context for people's growth, evolution, and flourishing—and that such personal development may be the secret weapon for business success in the future," wrote Robert Kegan and Lisa Lahey, professors at Harvard University, in their book *An Everyone Culture.*

What about business success *now?* I think companies should focus on hiring people with the best skills to do the jobs at hand so the *business* can prosper rather than worrying about a person's potential to "grow." Kegan disagrees.

"In a DDO, if you can perform the job the minute we give it to you, that's an error. That's a bad match. In a DDO you want a person who has the ability to learn and grow when the job is really over their heads. We expect them to initially fail and need support to develop the capacities that will enable them to do the job."

He likens the process to "a tow rope—you hold on initially for dear life and then eventually it will pull you up the mountain into a better version of yourself."

When it comes to personal and professional growth, I believe it can't be forced, that it happens organically from experience. You face challenges every day and learn to overcome them. Kegan says DDOs don't "wait around for those things to happen. They intentionally build them into their cultures." He admits this obsessive focus on development is not right for every company.

Another big thing in development today is "mentoring." I have always felt that "mentors"—people you want to emulate because you have so much fucking respect for them—are among the strongest influencers of one's organic growth.

Of course, even this concept has been bastardized and complicated by corporate wonks who have turned mentoring into yet another formal process, complete with rules and advice if you want to do it right. *Forbes, Harvard Business*

Review, and other business publications feature as many articles on mentoring as they do on hiring and performance reviews.

"Mentorship is a vital component of professional development," states Forbes in an article on the "Do's and Don'ts of Mentoring." When I look up "vital" in Webster's, it defines it as "necessary to the maintenance of life." That's pretty important. The Forbes article goes on to say, "Perhaps no business leader has reached success without the benefit of a mentor to guide him or her through the inevitable peaks and valleys of business."

This could be true. I had a mentor who greatly influenced my career. But there was only one and he was not forced on me through a formal mentoring program. This is not to say there weren't many supervisors, executives, colleagues, and other professionals I respected greatly, and I probably learned something from all of them. But there was really only one person I would consider a mentor.

Shortly after surviving Baxter's second restructuring in my tenure—the one that resulted in me being promoted to Director of Internal Communication—I began reporting to a VP of Communications named Phil Smith. His father had been a reporter for the Chicago Sun-Times who covered the Richard Speck mass murder case in the 1960s. Phil also had been a newspaper reporter early in his career.

When Baxter acquired American Hospital Supply in 1986, Phil came over from the American side, where he had been speechwriter for American Chairman and CEO Karl Bays. After the carnage of the 1989/90 restructuring, Phil took over as head of Corporate Communications for Baxter, and I began reporting to him.

At that point, more than ten years into my career, I thought I was pretty hot shit. I'd done pretty well for myself so far and just survived another restructuring at Baxter, even getting promoted. I certainly thought I was a good writer. But once I started working for Phil, I realized I'd somehow gotten this far without really knowing what the fuck I was doing.

Phil taught me to be a better writer. He taught me that effective writing is all in the reporting. The gathering of facts is what's most important. Let the facts tell the story. If you need to use a lot of adjectives, you don't have enough facts. He challenged me to meet very high standards. I can't believe I wrote for a living before Phil. I know I didn't start winning awards until after Phil.

But it was Phil's judgment, temperament, and decision-making that I admired most. Very cool, collected, and non-emotional; incomparably rational and informed; totally confident, and always right. Even people who didn't like him—people intimidated by his intelligence, ethics, and talent—still respected him. To this day, when I'm faced with a decision, I often think, *What would Phil do?* That's a mentor. That's a mensch. I've always tried to live up to his standards.

A *Harvard Business Review* article noted that mentoring is not the same as coaching, although both "are incredibly valuable in providing developmental support." Phil would have deleted the word "incredibly" and challenged *HBR* to *show* how valuable mentoring and coaching are!

Forbes listed "having a formal mentoring program" as the first "Do" in its "Do's and Don'ts" of mentoring. "That means participants agree to a realistic schedule and, as much as possible, stick to an agenda when they meet." Such a program includes goal-setting and frequent checkpoints to assess progress.

One business consultant suggests that men should seek a female mentor in the workplace. "There's a lot of talk about women mentoring younger women, but I think women need to mentor men as well," she said. "If I were a man who saw a personal, moral, or business reason to support gender diversity in my workplace, I would go to a female colleague and ask her to mentor me."

Gender awareness is a good thing. For example, I did a little research and learned that women speak, on average, 250 words a minute—about twice as much as men. If only I'd known this sooner. It could have had a major impact on my career.

Seriously, I can't imagine asking anyone of any gender to mentor me. I believe in humility but self-respect is important too. It just seems so subjugating. Go ahead and use the person as a role model. Ask them questions. Follow their example. But Phil never knew he was my mentor. I didn't even realize it until years later.

You never stop learning, folks—inside or outside of corporate walls. Take each experience, add it to your own personal inventory of knowledge, and use it to continue to grow. You can do whatever you want. It's entirely up to you. Just be true to yourself and try to enjoy the ride. All the rest is … well, you know.

EPILOGUE

There is so much Corporate Crap I didn't touch on. It's not that I'm lazy. My last book was 400 pages. It's that I think this subject is best covered in small bites—both in chapter length and number of topics—or it ceases to be fun.

We need to have more fun in our lives, and that includes at work. Easy for me to say with most of the Corporate Crap from my professional life safely in the rearview mirror. But it's hard. And some of the things I didn't touch on are some of the most serious workplace issues.

I didn't really touch on gender bias and sexual harassment. Gender-related issues have gotten more complicated as awareness of the needs of the transgender population has grown. Besides decisions on which bathroom some people can use, corporate bias against members of the LBGT community is as strong as bias against ethnic minorities and women in the struggle for equal pay, treatment, and opportunities.

Awareness of sexual harassment has grown, particularly in recent years with a slew of high-profile cases and the emergence of the #MeToo movement. But it remains an issue. Sexual harassment has gone on since the caveman. Yet many men, and even some women, have not evolved enough to make it extinct.

There is one incident I will relate just because it was so bizarre and brazen. It was in the late 1980s or early 1990s. A female coworker of mine was in the executive break room when the corporate officer in charge of our department confronted her and made some sexist remarks. He then took out a dildo and tossed it at her, giggling like a frat boy, like it was some big joke. This guy was a corporate VP, reporting directly to the CEO. My coworker told the CEO what happened. The CEO reamed frat boy a new asshole. But the guy kept his job.

I also didn't talk about drug testing. This was a bigger deal back when marijuana was illegal everywhere and in every instance. Today if you test positive for pot, it could be because it's prescribed or you live in a state where it's legal. When I was working in corporations, you could lose your job—even an office job that didn't require driving a car or working with machinery—if you tested positive for pot that may have been in your system from the previous weekend.

I was going to devote a chapter to "Corporate Crap in the Retail Sector" but soon realized this requires a book of its own—*Corporate Crap: Retail Edition*. My wife has been a retail store manager her whole life. Managers of department stores, mall outlets, specialty shops—any retail establishment that deals directly with the public—have unique challenges. For them, the "corporate office" is an ivory tower in some faraway place where people in suits making a lot more money and who have never waited on a customer in their lives try to tell them how to do their jobs.

The stories my wife brings home daily (she is currently a manager at our local Target) are enough to make you hate your fellow man. Shoplifters are such scum. Most don't even steal out of need. They simply feel entitled to take shit that doesn't belong to them so the rest of us have to pay higher prices. When they get caught, they're indignant, like *their* rights have been violated. My wife lost her job once when she caught a shoplifter who complained to the corporate office that she'd been "profiled." This person had been caught red-handed stealing merchandise from the store! But she was black and my wife is white and the company feared a lawsuit, so they fired my wife.

Besides dealing with shoplifters, retail store managers are forced to hire the least dependable employees in the workforce. They can only offer so much in wages to hourly workers, most of whom are part time and do not plan to make this their career. Throw in things like employee theft, rude customers, corporate wonks who send the wrong signage and impose rules that don't make sense at the store level—not to mention the "e-shopping" trend that is slowly but surely putting retail establishments out of business—and it's no wonder that companies in retail routinely rank among America's worst companies to work for.

If you learned anything from this book, I hope it was that you should not let frustration with the corporate life get you down. Don't let it eat at you. Don't let it keep you up at night. No matter how much you hate your boss or your job, rise above it. Do what you need to do for yourself. Do what you need to do to keep your sanity. Laugh at the nonsense if you can. Pursue new opportunities with abandon if you must. There are a lot of ways to make a living. Maintain your self-respect. You'll feel better about yourself, and when that happens, you're usually more successful. I wish you luck. And thanks for reading my book.

ACKNOWLEDGEMENTS

I want to thank Kelly Leonard and Steve Kakos of Second City Works for taking time out of their busy schedules to sit with me and share their insights on many of the topics covered in this book. I want to thank everyone who responded to my online solicitations for examples of personal experiences in the various areas of Corporate Crap I wrote about. (You have my sympathy.) I want to thank all the Human Resource managers, business consultants, researchers and other professionals whose opinions and data I quoted in the text, culled from the vast archives of business literature on these various topics. Finally, to reinforce what I said in the *Dedication*, I want to thank all my former bosses, coworkers, employees, clients, CEOs, business partners, and everyone else with whom I've worked over the past forty years. Each of you contributed something to this book. I appreciate all the experiences, good and bad, that shaped my career in the corporate world. I wish all of you continued success in pursuit of your goals.

DEC -- 2018

CPSIA information can be obtained
at www.ICGtesting.com
Printed in the USA
FFHW011255301118
49721160-54142FF

9 781457 566141